Challenge and Change

The Travails and Joys of a Complex Woman

ALLEN HERN

 FriesenPress

One Printers Way
Altona, MB R0G 0B0
Canada

www.friesenpress.com

I am indebted to Erin Linn McMullan for her editing of "Challenge and Change
-the Travails and Joys of a Complex Woman."

I also appreciate the proofreading/editing of my wife Sheila Hern and my
daughter, Juanita Stauffer.

ISBN
978-1-03-913784-4 (Hardcover)
978-1-03-913783-7 (Paperback)
978-1-03-913785-1 (eBook)

1. BIOGRAPHY & AUTOBIOGRAPHY, RELIGIOUS

Distributed to the trade by The Ingram Book Company

Challenge and Change

Foreword:

For many years, during her time in Nassau in the Bahamas, Reba Hern encouraged the members of my family to visit her in her Island home. None of us ever did. I wish we had done so. It would have been great to see her teaching her Bahamian students. But it didn't happen.

She was a fascinating woman, this cousin of mine.

When she died, she left behind almost 40 journals of her life, of her service and of her world travels.

Reba's journals were written over a time span of 75 years from age 16 to age 91. Most are from her time in Nassau through to the years before her death in the year 2000. Those chronicles reveal the various aspects of her personality and character of which we in the family were not aware.

Written in a rather cramped handwriting, they are not easy to decipher, but they record, in detail, her thoughts and her observations, whether describing her experiences as a young woman growing up in Sault Ste. Marie, Ontario, or as the second woman to be ordained into the ministry of the United Church of Canada, or as a worker with the Catholic Children's Aid Society, or as a teacher of Religious Knowledge and English in Nassau, or in her extensive travels.

To read one of her day-by-day records is to be there with her, to see what she saw, to experience what she experienced and to enter into her feelings, whether positive or negative.

Those memoirs convinced me that there was a story worth sharing in these pages and there's no time like the present to share it.

She lived in Nassau at a time when the Bahamas were on the cusp of independence and when a great deal of change was taking place. Her own independent spirit found a reflection in their transforming journey from colonialism to independence from British rule, from the governmental control of the white 'Bay Street boys' to the trial-and-error government of the black majority.

In 2018, eighteen years after she passed away, my wife and I visited Nassau to help us better understand Reba's life, and viewed for ourselves the city in which she spent 16 years.

Traveling by taxi, by water taxi, and by bus, we got an overview of the city. Better than that was the joy of meeting with Dr. Gail Saunders and Dr. Nicolette Bethel who were able to help us to see the Bahamas as she would have known them and meeting at least one person who remembered her from her days at the Government High School. Our visit also opened the door to people's memories, and to a number of new friends.

I am Reba's first cousin, newly retired after 50 years in pastoral ministry and rejoicing to share with you the story of a woman ahead of her times.

Join with me, then, as we explore the travails and joys of this complex woman.

Preface to "Challenge and Change: The Travails and Joys of a Complex Woman"

It has been a privilege to write this memoir of my cousin Reba Hern. Her story needs to be told.

I want to pay tribute to my editor, Erin McMullen, who has laboured long to help get this story into print. Her help and advice have been invaluable. Thank you, Erin.

I also want to pay tribute to my wife, Sheila, for her patience and perseverance in reading and rereading the manuscript. Whereas I ask her to 'read for content', the first thing she sees on the page is the glaring error that my typing or spelling or grammar or punctuation has slipped in without my awareness. Interesting that she sees still more of these miscues in second or third reading. I am indebted to her. Thank you, Sheila.

May I include a disclaimer for the reader? I ask you to take note of the fact that the author has been a pastor for over fifty years. Perhaps you may pardon the fact that I write from an evangelical Christian perspective which did not reflect the religious leanings of all my relatives, and may not be the mindset of all my readers.

I am also indebted to my brother Gordon for the helpful memories which he contributed.

I wish I wish I had written before my oldest brother died suddenly. No nursing home for him, but a great loss to one who would tell Reba's story.

Allen Hern October, 2021

CHAPTER ONE

Welcome to a New World

**"Life is what happens to us while we are making
other plans."**

— Allen Saunders

Her new home!

As the old T.C.A. plane descended, Reba Hern caught her first glimpse of the land that was to be her new home.

The plane which carried her was a Canadair North Star plane which was in use by Trans Canada Airlines from 1946 into the mid-sixties. Its Rolls-Royce engines achieved a cruising speed of 325 mph while carrying 52 passengers - not a very large plane and noted as being noisy.

Reba wrote in her journal, "My seat was opposite the wing. I felt a bit apprehensive because it was a strange new experience to be on a plane as it taxied down the runway and lifted into the air. It wasn't an experience that I looked forward to or wanted, but under the circumstances it seemed the best."

"Approaching our destination at around 6 p.m. EDT (Eastern Daylight Time) we saw the first of the Bahamas. Looking down from the plane into the clear blue, even turquoise waters of the Atlantic Ocean, I began to see the first of the Bahama Islands in the midst of an endless ocean. We passed over one fairly large one with well-marked roads and what seemed a fair-sized village. It was probably the island of Abaco. We were told we were approaching Nassau."

In a few minutes, she looked down on a flat island with two large lakes in the middle. As they began to descend, she experienced a mixture of fear, excitement, and apprehension as she watched the ground rushing up toward them. The plane landed safely and taxied to a stop at the Oakes Airfield, "an old, shabby airport."

Gathering herself and her handbag, she stepped out into the oppressive heat of Nassau in the Bahamas. It was September 5, 1957.

The question that was uppermost in Reba's mind was, "What am I doing here?"

The answer to that question is worthy of our attention.

Reba Hern was a woman who was often on the cusp of change. In 1925, she was a naïve sixteen-year-old girl observing the formation of the United Church of Canada. In 1937, she was the second woman ordained to the ministry of the United Church of Canada. In 1957, she was arriving in Nassau, the Bahamas, to begin a new life as a teacher at the very moment which Sir Randol Fawkes described as "the beginning of the end of British colonialism, white supremacy, and racial discrimination." [1]

Reba continues, "I got through Customs flying when I said I had come to teach at the Government High School. As I entered the waiting area, I found the headmaster of the Government High School, Dr. and Mrs. Peggs, and Miss Margaret Hyslop waiting for me. Leaving the airport, they drove me along an avenue lined with palm trees to Hoffer's Guest House where I had a room for the night."

She was in an entirely new environment, unlike anything she had experienced in Canada. Her first impressions of her new area: "It is very hot in Nassau. The heat met me like a blanket when I stepped off the plane. At night, I slept without even a sheet over me."

As she settled into her temporary home, some of her new teacher friends took her for a picnic at Love Beach.

"The water at Nassau is very salty and very, very clear. There are many fish in the water and with goggles you can see very well underwater. The sand is a pulverized rock and sticks to you, but is very clean. It is hot, and the water is

---

1   Randol Fawkes, founder of the Bahamas Federation of Labor and the acknowledged leader of Bahamian Trade Unionists. Michael Craton and Gail Saunders, *Islanders in the Stream: A History of the Bahamian People, Volume 2* (University of Georgia Press, 1998), p. 309.

as if it had been heated. Leaving the water, it was a little too hot on the beach so we all sat under a big sea grape tree."

Almost at once she was thrust into her new role as a teacher. With Margaret, she visited the Government High School for the first time. "The boys' uniforms were bright blue shirts and white pants; the girls' uniforms were bright blue jumpers and white blouses. They were all spotlessly clean and looked very nice."

"On this first day, there was an assembly followed by teaching two or three classes. As I had no idea what I am to teach them, all I could do was talk to them. It was a unique experience to stand before all these coloured faces.

"The school is very poor. The main building is an old Methodist Chapel. The partitions only go partway up and are so poor you can hear everything that is going on in all the rest of the building and there are six classes in progress all at once."

Reba was not wrong about the conditions at the Government High School.

In their book, *Islanders in the Stream*, authors Michael Craton and Gail Saunders tell us, "Although steadily enlarged, the Government High School remained in cramped non-purpose-built quarters until 1960 with a white headmaster of the old colonial stamp, and expatriate British and Canadian teachers rigidly constrained by Colonial Office regulations."[2]

Without doubt that 'headmaster of the old colonial stamp' was Dr. Peggs and Reba was one of the Canadian expatriate teachers.

On September 13, Reba wrote, "Today I finished my first week of teaching. As the weather has been dreadfully hot, I have found it to be very trying and I am a bit down. With this job, there are several unfavourable things. There is a definite cleavage between Dr. Peggs and his staff. None of them like him. Some are going out of their way to find things to criticize. Conditions are far from ideal but why not make the best of it?"

I suspect that Dr. Peggs was a very English gentleman. Surprisingly, Reba was invited from time to time to the Peggs' home, "a large Spanish style house arranged around a garden in the centre. While magnificent in the half-light, it is not so good in the full light. It is in poor condition with cracks and breaks in plaster and glass. The living room has a huge bay window which overlooks the sea, which rolls right up to the walls of the house." Obviously, the Peggs

---

2   Craton and Saunders, *Islanders in the Stream*, p. 306.

felt comfortable with this new teacher from Canada. Perhaps they found a warmth and acceptance in her which was lacking in other staff members.

At the end of a second week: "I have now been teaching for two weeks and I feel a good bit better about everything. This is an easy staff to feel at home with. I have adjusted much quicker than I did at the Catholic Children's Aid Society."

She lists the staff and their responsibilities and includes herself as "R.K."

I was at a loss to understand what subject R.K represented, until I came to understand that the letters stood for Religious Knowledge. With her background training in the ministry, and then as a worker in ministry to children and their families, it would seem that she would be well suited to this position. In addition, she would also teach English.

Still, I am left with a question: How did Reba come to the decision to leave Canada to teach in the Government High School in Nassau, the Bahamas? I think I know what led up to it. Thirteen years as the second ordained woman minister in Canada; the frustrations of being a woman in an 'old Boy's Club'; five years in a Catholic convent recovering from what I suspect was a case of burnout. Perhaps, too, there was a strained relationship with her parents, especially in their inability to understand her leaving the ministry and entering a convent.

I believe that she may have come to Nassau with a heavy heart, her early evangelical idealism broken, her denominational beliefs confused between Protestant or Catholic, and with a great need to fit in and to be accepted.

Now, here she is, starting all over again, in a new job, in a new culture, in a new country. Is this the explanation she would give, if she were here to tell her own story? I'm not sure. There is mystery here, even though we have more written records of this part of her life than for any other.

What she did not yet know, Reba had come to the Bahamas at a pivotal moment. Breaking new ground seems to have been her experience. As she had found herself at the forefront of the ordination of women in 1937, so now, at 48 years of age, she arrived in Nassau at the very moment when major changes were in the making.

As she walked along the waterfront on November 17, 1957, a scant two months after arriving, she received her first viewpoint of the racial tensions present in Nassau.

"As I took a good look at the fishing boats, I came to one unpainted boat whose owner was standing on the wharf and ready to talk. He was a coloured person[3] with a black velvet beret on his head and his pants rolled up one leg higher than the other.

"The boat belongs to a group of coloured people who live a very independent existence. Food is hominy grits and fish. They grind the corn. They grow their little bits of produce or catch some fish and bring it to sell at the market in Nassau. This is an existence but not a good life. There is no care of the aged at all. Those who have no relatives are in a sad plight.

"A soft-spoken and cultured man was also on the dock. The cultured black Bahamian was a speaker for the Progressive Liberal Party (PLP), which champions the rights of the coloured people and the underdog. 80% of the Bahamians are coloured and are controlled by the tiny minority of whites with their businesses on Bay Street.

"Our PLP man began to point out the gross injustice being done to these people. In the Bahamas, there is no income tax and no property tax but there is a tax on food and clothing.

"Thus, the rich avoid taxes and the burden of taxation falls on the poor. The 'Bay Street boys' hold a monopoly here and have fooled the out-islands. They give a little charity, send out a doctor, and distribute drinks at election time so the poor out-islander thinks they are interested in him and are his friend. But they have really kept the out-islander in poverty while they continue to grow rich themselves. The only out-island that has its eyes open is Andros. It alone returned two PLP men to the House of Assembly in the last election."

The cultured man to whom Reba was speaking turned out to be none other than Lynden Pindling, who had become the leader of the Progressive Liberal Party in 1955.

Saunders and Craton state that, "By 1953, [4]moves were afoot to organize a formal political party to oppose Bay Street and its practices, though the

---

3   Throughout the book, I have used the terms coloured, blacks and Negro when quoted as they were used in Reba's journals and by Dr. Gail Saunders in *Islanders in the Stream*.

4   Craton and Saunders, *Islanders in the Stream*, p. 307.

opposition remained weakened by lack of cohesion and concerted aims." Several attempts failed.

Much better organized,[5] with a well-formulated platform that addressed burning issues in a calm and deliberate manner, was the Progressive Liberal Party, the formation of which was announced late in October, 1953.

As expressed by Rev. H. H. Brown, "The Progressive Liberal Party hopes to show that your big man and your little man, your black, brown, and white man of all classes, creed, and religions in this country can combine and work together in supplying sound and successful political leadership which has been sadly lacking in the Bahamas."[6]

"The party's policy statement in June, 1954 called for wider representation in the House of Assembly, the enfranchisement of women…. It pledged support for equal employment opportunities, better education, lower prices, low-cost housing, and strong immigration controls." Yet despite its broad-based appeal, the PLP made slow progress at first.

"The two key figures were Milo Butler, the emotive Baptist-preacher style, and the more cerebral Lynden Pindling, who recognized that besides appealing to the oppressed black majority, a successful opposition party would have to mobilize a Bahamian Proletariat."

Michael Craton and Gail Saunders tell us that Lynden Pindling [7]was one of the outstanding alumni of the Government High School who had trained in England as a lawyer. This, of course was the school to which Reba has now come.

"Returning home in 1953, Pindling found neither rich briefs nor official employment and turned instead to litigation on behalf of poor clients and to popular politics. Pindling was to become the first black premier and prime minister."

"With the small PLP group acting for the first time as a coherent parliamentary opposition, the Bay Street clique was constrained to organize itself as a political party, though its United Bahamian Party (UBP) [8]was not formally constituted until March 1958."

---

5   Ibid, p. 308.

6   Ibid, p. 304.

7   Ibid.

8   Craton and Saunders, *Islanders in the Stream*, p. 310.

Thus, within six months of arriving, Reba found herself in a changing situation. At this point, her sympathies definitely lay with the Bahamian people. As she becomes better acquainted with her new home, we shall watch to see to what degree this continues.

As I read her journal about her early days in Nassau, I desired to learn more about her adopted country. In this, *Islanders in the Stream* proved to be so very helpful, adding to and clarifying my cousin's journal entries. I learned about the background of the Government High School. I learned that education in the Bahamas "was originally designed to provide minimal literacy and sound moral teaching rather than social mobility or even useful skills."

In fact, "there was no government secondary education whatsoever until the foundation of the Government High School in 1925."

Saunders and Craton state that, "the failure to promote popular education beyond the primary level, indeed, was the worst indictment against the Bahamian regime."

The authors indicate that although opening its doors to all classes and both sexes, "GHS was held back by the favour shown by most members of the government to Queen's College. It was also held back by its ability to attract only the sons of the poorest whites, and virtually no white girls."

To gain some further idea of Reba's new home we find that the Bahamas[9] consist of more than 700 islands, of which 10 or 11 are inhabited. The largest island is Andros Island. Other inhabited islands include Eleuthera, Cat Island, Long Island, San Salvador Island, Acklins, Crooked Island, Exuma, Berry Islands, and Mayaguana.

When Reba arrived in the Bahamas in 1957, the population was just over 100,000 with the majority of those living on the 21-mile-long New Providence Island.

Nassau, the capital city of the Bahamas, lies on this island with neighbouring undeveloped Hog Island, accessible via Nassau Harbor Bridge. Hog Island was soon to be rechristened and developed as Paradise Island after its world-famous Paradise Beach.

The city has a hilly landscape and is known for beaches as well as its offshore coral reefs, popular for diving and snorkelling. It retains many of

9   The Official Site of The Bahamas | It's Better In The Bahamas https://www. bahamas.com/

its typical pastel-coloured British colonial buildings, like the pink-hued Government House.

The harbour attracted settlers in the early days, particularly pirates. In fact, Nassau's population consisted mainly of pirates until 1718, when the Bahamas' first Royal Governor, Woodes Rogers expelled them, restored order, and built Fort Nassau. The Bahamas for centuries adopted Rogers' motto, "*Expulsis Piratis, Restituta Commercia*," which means, "Pirates Expelled, Commerce Restored." Now, 212,000 people call New Providence Island home, with a large portion of them residing in Nassau.

As we look at the map, we can't help but notice that Grand Bahama Island, Abaco, and Andros Island are far larger than New Providence. In fact, New Providence appears tiny by comparison. Nonetheless, it is on New Providence that the city of Nassau, the capital of the Bahamas, is located. The other islands are spoken of as "Out Islands".

All the islands are low and flat, with ridges that usually rise no more than 15 to 20 metres (49 to 66 feet).

The entire archipelago lies in the Atlantic Ocean and is located north of Cuba and Hispaniola (Haiti and the Dominican Republic); northwest of the Turks and Caicos Islands; southeast of the US state of Florida and east of the Florida Keys.

With this background, I want to take one more look at this woman who was brave enough to tackle such a new situation.

She was quite a woman, was my cousin Reba. A complex woman!

Now, what do I mean by that? My thesaurus states that this refers to a combination of emotions and impulses of which a person may not be aware but which still influences his or her behaviour. As I have read what Reba wrote about herself, I have come to believe that there were deep-rooted and sometimes conflicting feelings, which definitely influenced her outlook on life and on the reactions of other people. Yes, I believe there was complexity in this woman. But then, I think that there is a certain sense in which complexity seems to be the nature of the gender.

So, come with me as we discover "Nassau in a time of change."

Chapter Two

Nassau in a Time of Change

**"I can be changed by what happens to me but I refuse
to be reduced by it."**

— Maya Angelou

Before we go further with Reba's story, I would like you to meet her as a
person. At five feet, five inches tall, Reba had an 'air of authority'. Her round
face, with a florid complexion, was often wreathed in a warm smile, though
sometimes reflecting a quizzical, questioning expression.

With her dark hair piled high on her head, she maintained the same
general appearance through her many years in ministry, her years of teaching
in Nassau, her various passport photos, and her years in retirement.

Her voice was husky, but with a high-pitched tone, and her laughter was
something to be remembered. With her eyes crinkled with humour, her
laughter was a mixture of a hoo-hoo, and a kind of a snort. Often wiping her
hand across her face she displayed her beautiful ring.

To anyone meeting her, she was warm and friendly, but behind the outward
appearance there was a mind which was questioning, analyzing, and sometimes
criticizing. I did not realize that until reading her thoughts in her many journals.

As I have said, she was a complex woman with a keen, enquiring mind,
with which she drew her own conclusions; opinions not always in step with
the thoughts and ideas of others.

In visiting with my nieces and nephews in the Thessalon, Bruce Mines,
and Sault St. Marie areas of northwestern Ontario, who had only seen her in
her periodic visits, I was surprised to find that they all remembered her. With

one accord, they described her as someone who had a "presence" when she walked into a room. They all remember feeling that presence.

By November of 1957, Reba found herself embroiled in the racial tensions, which were stirring in Nassau.

"There is really a situation developing here in the Bahamas," she wrote, "The coloured people resent this little group of whites hogging everything and the whites refuse to face the issue. To them, the coloured people are an inferior breed who don't deserve any more than they get. There is a complete cleavage between the two.

"Nassau has just finished building a beautiful new airport at Windsor Field. There has developed a lot of trouble between the taxi drivers and a man called Dan Knowles. He runs a lot of limousines and buses."

Tensions were rising, but as school closed for the Christmas break in that first year, 1957, she took her first trip abroad, travelling to Jamaica with her friend Chris Davies, aboard the Royal Mail cargo vessel.

I don't expect that a mail vessel was any luxury liner. Still, as her 12-day trip begins, she reports: "A pleasant day at sea."

Sailing past the island of San Salvador, the island that was discovered by Columbus, past the tip of Cuba, Haiti and the Dominican Republic, they arrived in Kingston.

Their first short time was spent in the YWCA, a poor building but adequate. "Kingston is a very slummy place. All the better class live in the hills, so the city itself is very unattractive. We sat down under a tree in a grubby little park and several beggars approached us so we had to leave."

Deciding to leave the city, they were taken to Bamboo Lodge in the Blue Mountains to a bungalow named Hibiscus with a lovely view: out over the hills right across the Kingston harbour.

"The seven acres of the Bamboo Lodge are beautiful, on which they grow oranges, grapefruit, lemons, limes, guavas, breadfruit, bananas, coffee, pineapple, paw paws, and coconuts. The poinsettia are beautiful, especially two large bushes as you come along the lane. They have a swimming pool and shuffleboard.

"I had thought that in Jamaica I would find lots of fruit and vegetables but not in these stores. The natives live in small, very poor houses all up and down the hills. We walked as far as the post office, a small poor affair. In all my life, I have never seen smaller, poorer places. These people have no bus service of any kind. Their only transport is the few donkeys they have. They put two big baskets over each side and sit in front. Thus, they bring their staples from Kingston. There must be a great deal of malnutrition."

On December 20, Reba flew home from Jamaica to Nassau. "Kay and Joyce were at the airport to meet me. It was good to be back to Nassau amongst people I know. Christmas is a time when you want to be amongst people who are well known."

And so, Reba completed her first term in her new land. All in all, she appears to have been adjusting well to the new culture, to the new challenge, and the great change. She was also beginning a pattern of travel that would take her to many lands during coming years.

As Reba began her second term at the Government High School in Nassau, she had opportunity to reflect on the changes that had taken place in her life.

"How different my life from what it was last year. Last year, my social life consisted of going to Aunt Minnie's in Ontario for a lovely dinner and a pleasant evening of music with cousin Harold, going to a few shows, and going to Wilbur and Carrie's (her twin sister) for the weekend.

"When I visited with them, we mostly sat around and did nothing except attending church on Sunday. It was nice being with Carrie, but those weekends were boring, and we were much too critical of our relatives. We spent too much time pointing up the failures in other people."

Here we catch a glimpse of the differences between the two sisters. Carrie's was a much more conventional life – married to a minister rather than being one; a stay-at-home mother of two daughters, Carol Ann and Brenda, living in Erindale, near Toronto. Reba's was a more adventurous life – first in becoming a woman minister in the United Church of Canada, then a resident in a Catholic convent. Then a children's worker, and now a teacher in a new land, and a world traveller.

Is it possible that each of them may have envied what the other had?

Reba's life was certainly different, and she exposes something of her true feelings in this journal entry.

But Reba was no longer living a quiet life in Ontario. Unknowingly, she had been thrust into the Bahamas at a time of social upheaval and change.

In some ways, we see a parallel between the upheaval in Nassau and the upheaval in her own life.

As 1958 began, the tensions of November boiled over.

An excellent Internet article: 'The 1958 General Strike and the Making of the Modern Bahamas' by Larry Smith[10] bore out Reba's claims.

"By 1958 the classic battle lines were drawn between an unyielding authoritarian, monopolistic business elite (who happened to be white), and a majority of deprived citizens who yearned for democracy and social change (who happened to be black).

"The stage was set for major conflict. The British governor at the time described the ruling elite (which later constituted itself as the United Bahamian Party) as 'recalcitrant, stubborn and politically obtuse...not very numerous, but extremely powerful in the material sense and pretty unscrupulous.' They maintained their control over the electorate by bribery, intimidation and restriction of the franchise. Women could not vote, but property owners - many of whom were white, certainly could.

"Black Bahamians had been operating taxis since the 1930s, picking up cruise passengers from Prince George Wharf and air passengers from Oakes Field.

"The opening of Nassau's international airport in November 1957 was a significant event accompanied by an even more significant display of greed and political stupidity."

He then goes on to speak of a group of major hotels which proposed to sign an exclusive agreement with a new taxi company set up by Bobby Symonette, the son of government leader Roland Symonette.

"The 200 taxi drivers were understandably outraged. So, on November 2 and 3 they blocked the airport with their cars, forcing airlines to cancel flights. The blockade was supported by airport workers who were part of the Bahamas Federation of Labor."

It came to a head when Sir Randol Fawkes and Lynden Pindling gave the word, which led workers everywhere to walk off their jobs. Hotels closed and the city came to a standstill. The governor called for a warship and British

---

10 www.bahamapundit.com 2012/01/ "the 1958 general strike and the making of the modern Bahamas.html/

troops arrived from Jamaica to reinforce the 300 policemen, whose loyalty could not be guaranteed.

"The 1958 general strike has been called one of the seminal events of the modern Bahamas. The tragedy of it is that all this unnatural hatred has been produced by the greed and avarice of a few men in the community."

According to Fawkes, their action marked "the beginning of the end of British colonialism…white supremacy and racial discrimination."

Meanwhile, Reba was seeing the effects of the strike right in the home of Florence, Doris, and Ethel Smith, three sisters who wanted to be considered white.

"The Smiths, with whom I live, are completely dominated by the Bay St. Boys. Yet everyone knows that in their background is coloured blood. Florie shows this very plainly.

"I have just listened to a terrible tirade by Florrie against the coloured people. If all the white Bahamians have the attitude of the Smiths, there will be serious trouble. I have never listened to such one-sided bitterness in my life as in this house tonight. A year ago, little did I think that I would be witnessing, at first hand, this horrid thing. My whole soul goes out to these so-called white people who so obviously have allowed themselves to become the tools of the powers of darkness."

Reba was not only observing this social upheaval in the home in which she was living. She also was able to observe the reaction at the Government High School. "At school, amongst educated people of culture, the story was different. They calmly accepted that the status quo has to come to an end. All that they feared was that the coloured people would try to act too fast."

The strike lasted only 19 days. By the end of January, Reba says everything seems to be back to normal. "The tension in the house is gone. Rumour has it that the strike is over, but no announcement. It was amazing the fear the strike aroused in the white Bahamians."

The following year saw extension of the franchise to all men over 21, and the creation of four new parliamentary seats (all of which were won by the PLP). The massive cultural shift as the Bahamas and its people work towards independence was on. As it progressed it would transform the Bahamas completely. It would take years to develop but it had begun.

Meanwhile, my cousin continued to enjoy the opportunity to check out new areas in the Bahamas.

On March 17, 1958 she wrote, "I had a very full weekend. Very early Eunice and I set off by plane for Eleuthera."

Eleuthera is an island in The Bahamas, lying 50 miles (80 km) east of Nassau. It is 110 miles (180 km) long and, in places, little more than 1 mile (1,600 m) wide.

"The pilot took us in turn into the cockpit. If you push the stick away from you the plane goes down, if toward you, it goes up. The plane held 16 people. It was really thrilling sitting in the cockpit of the plane. We had a nice view of Governor's Harbor, which is a pretty little town on the mainland. We arrived at Rock Sound about 9 and got off the plane. Mr. Kemp and Arthur Barnet were there to meet us. Mr. Kemp took us to a charming little house where we met Mrs. Kemp, had coffee and then set off for a drive in a half-ton truck. First, we saw the Cotton Bay Club, a large golf course and cottages and a long low clubhouse. It has a magnificent beach. Mr. Kemp told us that only very rich millionaires come here. Then he drove us through a little native village called Wyness Bight. The people seemed so dreadfully poor and their houses small shacks. As it was church time, we saw one or two churches with services in progress. They were the worst churches I have seen - mere unpainted shells with broken down wooden benches.

"What these people live on is a mystery to me.

"We passed through Fox Hill, Bannerman Town to the end of the Island. We passed one of the early plantations called Millers. The old plantation house is still there with walls two feet thick. The roads were built by slaves. At a small place called Green Castle, we saw some attempt to keep the houses up, a very attractive school and teachers' residence. At one, we got back to Rock Sound for dinner. The Kemp's kitchen is very attractive and spotlessly clean. The place is every inch a home. We had a wonderful dinner. Mr. Kemp then drove us to the lovely Rock Sound Club.

"On the way, we passed a farm with a great many Aberdeen Angus cattle. The club has a good garden, and a pawpaw tree with pawpaws right from the top to the ground. We had a short visit with the Barnetts and then a rush to the airport and away. It was a delightful day, but all too short."

As we have seen, Nassau was indeed in a time of change.

And so was Reba!

Chapter Three

The Complexity Begins

"From a little spark may burst a mighty flame."

— Dante

We've already found out that both Nassau and Reba were changing and we have met her as an adult in that situation, but, of course, Reba didn't start out that way. She has a history that has prepared the way for these later stages.

Let me take you back to the beginning.

In our family, we called her by a courtesy title, "Aunt Reba". She wasn't really my aunt. She was my cousin but, in many ways, she was more like an aunt than a cousin.

She was born in 1909; I was born in 1939. Thirty years' age difference is a lot to bridge, especially when one is young. She was already a young woman of 28 years old, serving in her first pastoral ministry for two years when I was born, so you can understand why she might have been "Aunt Reba" to me. Because the church she was serving was only 30 miles from our home, my brothers Norman, age thirteen, and Gordon, age seven had the opportunity to know her a little, but I have no memory of those years.

By the time my children came along, the term "aunt" was a courtesy title which we continued to use in our home, even though to my wife, Sheila and myself, she was just Reba.

It was January 31, 1909 when lovely little twin girls were born into the family of Herbert and Carrie Hern. Reba Ethel and Carrie Mildred Hern had arrived in the world. Although their pictures look so much alike in their childhood, especially when they were dressed alike, they must have been fraternal twins since their personalities seem to have been very different.

Reba and Carrie Hern - 6 Months

My dad was Lew Hern, Herb's younger brother. Dad married late, and I was his youngest, born when he was already 50 years old, so you can see how this age spread came about.

Reba's birth certificate and her passport says that the girls were born in Thessalon, Ontario, a little town on the north shore of Lake Huron, about 50 miles east of Sault Ste. Marie, Ontario. I, too, was born in Thessalon, on the family farm, but Uncle Herb had long since left the farm in favour of a job in the Pulp Mill in "the Soo," so I would have expected that the girls would be born in Sault Ste. Marie. Perhaps Herb and his wife, Carrie were still living in the Thessalon area when he was 29 years of age. The other possibility might be that Aunt Carrie returned to her family near Thessalon for the birth.

At any rate, from the time Reba was a young girl, the family was living at 157 Cathcart Street in Sault Ste. Marie, Ontario and the girls grew up in that lovely home.

Reba and Carrie – 3 years

"The Sault" or "The Soo" as it was known locally, was a small city of probably under 20,000 people in 1910. Incorporated in 1912, it had two main industries, the Algoma Steel Plant, in which my uncle, Lionel Keith was a foreman, and the Pulp Mill, in which Uncle Herb was a millwright.

Situated on the turbulent St. Mary's River, which joins Lake Superior and Lake Huron, the city is the site of the "Soo Locks" which lift oceangoing ships 23 feet in three stages from Lake Huron to Lake Superior. To the south, across the St. Mary's River is the United States of America and the city of Sault Ste. Marie, Michigan. Due to having the same name, these border towns are known locally as the twin cities; joined by the International Bridge, which connects Interstate 75 on the Michigan side and Huron Street on the Ontario side.

Since these locks also form the border between Sault, Ontario, and Sault, Michigan, the locks are parallel to each other with the southern locks being owned by the United States and the northern locks owned by Canada. The American locks are larger and accommodate oceangoing vessels while the Canadian locks carry smaller vessels.

Being a farm boy, it was exciting for me to visit our relatives who lived in "the city". There we visited Uncle Herb and Aunt Carrie, Uncle Lionel and Aunt Alice Keith, and Aunt Sadie, a spinster sister, who worked for the city.

The family had given Aunt Sadie the "privilege" of providing a home, first for her mother until she died, and then for her oldest sister, Eva, until she too died after years of dementia. As in many such situations, it became a question of whether the caregiver or the one cared for would succumb first.

On one of those rare occasions when we stayed overnight in the Sault, I remember waking up in the morning in Aunt Alice's tall old brick house on John Street. The sounds of the city traffic rushing by, and the sounds of the steel plant in the distance were very strange and exciting to a kid who was used to the quiet of the country. I don't remember ever staying over at Uncle Herb's.

To me, Uncle Herb and Aunt Carrie's was a much nicer home. In their living room was an attractive oval coffee table, with a blue Wedgewood candy dish sitting on an embroidered doily. On the wall above was a framed picture of the twin girls as young ladies. To me, 157 Cathcart was a real "city home".

Of course, Reba and her sister Carrie were not there when I was a child.

I know little of their childhood years but in 1925, when the girls were 16 years of age, Reba began to keep a journal in two little black notebooks. It took both to successively cover that one year.

But even before that we have some records of her childhood.

Reba and Carrie - 6 years

She tells of a trip to British Columbia that she and Carrie went on with their mother.

"When Carrie and I were children, mother had a plan whereby she would go out west every few years to see her sisters. Since she was the only one who had remained in Ontario, this was important to her.

"I remember one trip in particular when Carrie and I were little girls. We went down to the Sault Ste. Marie Government Dock and boarded a ship, probably in the early afternoon. Away we sailed - through the Locks and out onto the great Lake Superior. Toward evening we sat down to a magnificent dinner. The gleaming cutlery was lined out from our plates. We proceeded to enjoy a seven-course meal served in great style. I don't remember if mother ate all seven courses but I know I did. The next morning, we had another fancy meal - our leisurely breakfast. Then we got off at the Port Arthur dock and there, drawn up beside the dock, our train was waiting for us.

"Away we went, past the vast muskeg of north-western Ontario, then past the farms of Manitoba and across the great wide prairies. In Alberta, we began to see the foothills, then it was into the mountains, the beautiful Rockies. In Spence's Bridge, in British Columbia, mother and us girls got off. Aunt Lou was waiting for us with all her plans made to convey us to the cattle town of Merritt, British Columbia."

Merritt was a dusty little cattle town in the Nicola Valley in the south-central Interior of British Columbia, two hundred and seventy kilometers northeast of Vancouver. Situated at the confluence of the Nicola and Coldwater rivers, it bore even then a slight foretaste of the town which one finds today at the midway point between Hope and Kamloops on the fast-moving Coquihalla Highway.

"I don't know why Carrie and I were so captivated by cowboys, but we were. As we came into Merritt, we were so thrilled to see all these cowboys going about. In the center of the town there were a lot of posts with big rings in them where the cowboys tethered their horses. There were the cowboys themselves with their big hats and chaps. Some fellows wore leather, others wore woolly sheepskin chaps.

"Aunt Lou was not nearly as enthused about the cowboys as we children were and warned us that we must keep our distance. The cattle people were not Aunt Lou's cup of tea! Cowboys, ranchers, and ranchers' wives were in a different social class. She belonged to the elite of the town of Merritt. She was the matron of the hospital. Doctors and lawyers were her friends, not ranchers and their wives.

"One day, when we visited Aunt Lou at work, Carrie and I were walking down the corridor in the hospital. We came to a bay where those who were seated were waiting to see the doctor. To our great delight, here sat a cowboy, big hat in hand, clad in jeans, chaps and all. We stopped dead, hoping he would notice us. We would love to speak to him and ask him some questions. He was completely wrapped up in his own thoughts and didn't even seem to notice us. We were thrilled anyway and stood looking at him."

Can you picture these two little twin girls, perhaps seven or eight years of age, probably dressed alike in frilly dresses, and with their hair all curled looking with big eyes at this fascinating fellow?

"Later, with mother and Aunt Lou, we told them how thrilled we were to be so near to him. Aunt Lou told us he was in hospital because he had contracted an unpleasant disease. Carrie and I didn't know anything about unpleasant diseases. Aunt Lou then went on to tell us he was half Indian. Again, Aunt Lou missed the mark. We were being brought up by a mother who hadn't an ounce of snobbery in her and so far as racism, she wasn't the slightest bit interested in the word. For us, this simply made our hero much more exciting."

Reba goes on to tell of Aunt Lou's marriage to the owner of the drug store (quite a catch!), which didn't work out as well as her aunt had hoped.

I am sure that Aunt Carrie and the girls continued on to Vancouver to visit with other sisters, but nothing is said about that in her diary. The cowboy was her chief memory.

After their trip to British Columbia, Reba's journal picks up the story as the girls returned to 'the Soo.' What an interesting life these sisters were beginning.

As seen in Reba's journal, their lives really radiated around school and church. I would suggest that from a fairly early age Reba had a serious interest in spiritual things. I found within her papers a small card entitled "My Life Decision."

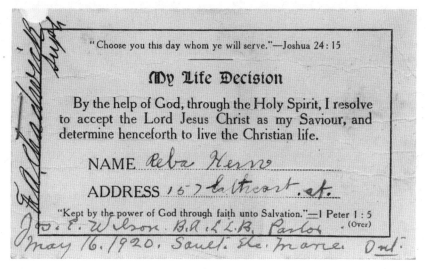

My Life Decision

On the front of the card was the following statement:

"By the help of God, through the Holy Spirit, I resolve to accept the Lord Jesus Christ as my Saviour and determine henceforth to live the Christian life."

She signed her name in a childish hand at 11 years of age. This card was also signed by the minister, Jos. E. W. Wilson, B.A. L.L.B, Pastor, Sault Ste. Marie, Ont., and by F.A. Chadwick, Superintendent, showing that this was not something that was done lightly or frivolously, but as a serious commitment. The date was May 16, 1920.

On the back of the card there are explanatory notes:

Four Steps into the Kingdom of God.

1. Repentance: Repentance is a turning from sin to God with a full purpose hereafter of doing His will. "I thought on my ways and turned my feet unto Thy testimonies." Psalm 119:59. See also Luke 15: 18, 19; Isaiah 55: 6, 7.

2. Confession: Confession is an acknowledgment of our sins to God with a desire for His forgiveness. "If we confess our sins, He is faithful and just to forgive our sins and to cleanse us from all unrighteousness." 1 John 1:9 See also Proverbs 28:13; Luke 18:13, 14.

3. Faith: Faith is believing in Christ as a personal Saviour and committing ourselves without reserve to Him and to His service. "But as many as received Him, to them He gave power to become the sons of God, even to them that believe on His name." John 1:12. See also John 3:16; Hebrews 7:25; Acts 4:12; Ephesians 1:7.

4. Obedience: Obedience is doing the will of God. This is required of all who belong to God's kingdom. "If you love me, keep my commandments." John 14:15; "As you have therefore received Christ Jesus the Lord, so walk in Him." Colossians 2:6. See also Matthew 22:37 - 39; 1 John 5:4, 5.

All these verses are well worth looking up and thinking about.

What this also shows is the tremendous importance of early Sunday School training. For many years Aunt Sadie conducted children's meetings after school in her home where a succession of boys and girls heard about God and the Lord Jesus Christ. We'll never know what lasting effect those gatherings had on the children. Sunday School teachers should also never despair of the value of those Bible stories in the lives of little ones. Aunt Sadie also subscribed to Christian children's magazines for me, which had an influence on my life, not only then, but also in later years.

Thus, we see that from an early age, Reba was learning about and choosing to follow the Lord Jesus as her Saviour and Lord. Here we see the birth of the faith that she would carry with her throughout her life. "Faith comes by hearing and hearing by the Word of God." Romans 10:17.

We shall see this reflected in her journal as we learn more about the twin girls at age 16. As I say, the church was very central in the development of the two girls. It is therefore not a great surprise that as an adult she felt led to pursue a Bachelor's degree and then to enroll in Emmanuel College, the United Church training school for United Church ministers.

How did that come about? That story is down the road but for now, it's enough to remark that the twins were the delight of their parents' hearts, and would remain that way, without any other brothers or sisters to share or detract from that special relationship.

CHAPTER FOUR

A Youthful Journal

"We cannot always build the future for our youth, but we can build our youth for the future."

— F. D. Roosevelt

As Reba and Carrie turned 16, I turn to two little black notebooks probably bought in the five and dime store long before K-mart or Wal-Mart. We might call them her diaries, or we can describe them as the first of her many journals.

The year of the writing of her thoughts in those little black notebooks is of importance to the story, for 1925 was the year in which the United Church of Canada was born as we learn from the innocent musings of a teenage girl jotting down the everyday events of her daily life. As yet, she had no idea of the conflict that that merger was going to bring into the life of herself and her sister.

Join me as we listen in on some of the thoughts of those carefree days.

May 8, 1925: "I went to school as usual with Carrie, Blanche, and Wilma. We had Gym first period. Things went as usual at school. After 4, five of us girls went picking flowers. We got home at 6:45 and had supper, then went out and played basketball till 9 o'clock."

Reba's journal chronicles her day-by-day activities: "I got up early to do my Botany class as I had a speech to give. The rest of the day went as all school days do go. In Latin period, Mrs. Thorn sent me to the blackboard and I got my work all right - only one mistake. Carrie was also sent and she got very nervous and had a hard time." This would seem to suggest that Reba was the more formidable of the twin girls, while Carrie was less sure of herself.

A few days later, she writes with a fountain pen, rather than the later ball-point pens with which we are so much more familiar: "Got up at 9 o'clock and spent the morning in getting up a Bible lesson for C.G.I.T. (Canadian Girls in Training) and playing hymns. We went to Sunday School in the afternoon. After Sunday School, Dorothy and I went for a walk down past the Post Office. After supper, we went to Central Church. The title of the sermon was, "The Wrath of God", a splendid sermon. The wrath of God is not really anger, but almost sadness. Mr. Colebrook sang and he is a wonderful singer."

Figure 5 Reba and Carrie - age 16

From this, it is easy to see that to read the 1925 diary of a youthful Reba Hern is to read the story of an average teenage girl in a time very different from that with which we, in the 21st century, are familiar. To catch just a glimpse of that difference, she tells of a trip to the farm, taking one dress, bloomers, and middies (a loosely fitting blouse with a sailor collar worn by women and children). Even trying to compare that description of the clothing of a 16-year-old girl with a 16-year-old dressed in today's fashions is impossible.

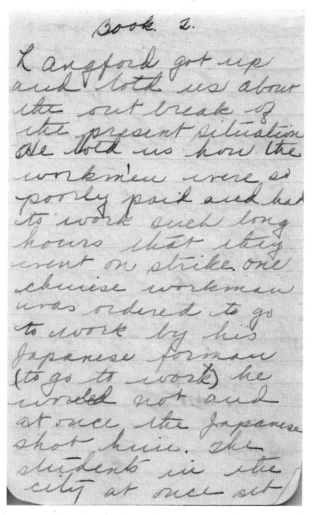

Reba's first journal - age 16

In another entry, Reba tells in typical youthful style, of attending a summer Bible camp near Bruce Mines, about 40 miles from the Soo.

Saturday: "After breakfast we sat around the tent, then played ball. After this Marjorie, Lilian, Carrie, and I went swimming. We did not stay in long as the water was cold. In the evening opening session, Mayor Grigg of Bruce Mines and Rev. J. Martin gave speeches. We got out of the meeting early and went to sleep on our rocky beds that were pitched on rough ground.

"On Sunday morning, having gotten dressed, we went to the morning service in the Bruce Mines United Church.

"Mr. Dyang, a Chinese student, took the missionary lecture. He told us of how China was anti-foreign, believing she was the greatest nation in the world and knowing nothing of the outside world. Mr. Langford got up and told us how the workmen were so poorly paid and had to work such long hours that they went on strike. One Chinese workman was ordered to go to work, by his Japanese foreman. He would not so the foreman shot him.

"The students in the city at once set up banners and marched through the streets telling of the terrible tragedy. The British officer ordered them to break it up, and when they would not, the officer ordered them to be fired on."

I am sure that this story made a great impact on a group of impressionable teens. Many years later, when she visited China, I am sure that this account still remained in Reba's memory.

In typical camper style, Reba tells of sports, staying up past curfew, of early morning prayer meetings. "Up at 6:00; prayer meeting 7:20, meetings." With delight, she reported on a ball game between the preachers and the campers. "The preachers were defeated."

Fri. July 31: last day: Morning Prayer; lectures; consecration service. "Cards were passed around and the spirit of Jesus seemed very, very near to us all indeed."

On Saturday, they took the boat home to the Sault but were sick all the way. Reba was to give a speech in church about the camp on Sunday but had little time to prepare and felt she could have done a lot better. Perhaps this is a foreshadowing of giving sermons in later years.

Little did she know that in a few years she would be a minister serving four churches not far from the Bruce Mines community.

As we continue to follow her youthful activities, music, and choir seems to have been important to the girls. "This evening was choir practice. Carrie and I went. We started right off with 'I will magnify Thee', which is a heavy anthem. Then we sang 'O clap your hands together'. The practice was a very heavy one for me and I was very tired before 10 o-clock when we got out."

At age 16, in the year 1925, Reba and her twin sister, Carrie did not sit around in the evening watching television, for that medium did not enter Canada until 1952. The first television studios were founded in Montreal and Toronto in that year. Nor is there any evidence in her two small notebook-sized journals of hanging out with boys. Instead, you find repeated descriptions of a variety of girls going on walks, playing basketball, learning to play baseball, and other innocent activities. "After Sunday School, in the afternoon, my friend Dorothy and I went for a walk down past the post office."

In those days, as in later times, one of the places of interest was the boat canal with the Locks lifting boats from Lake Huron up to Lake Superior or down the other way, which I have already described.

Reba tells of going for a walk after Sunday School with Marjorie and Carrie. "We went to the canal. We saw Bill Harris and Claude Elliot out in a boat. Soon Bill asked if we would like to go for a ride. I was not sure whether it was right or not, but both Carrie and Marjorie wanted to go, so I went. It can't be any worse than car riding and yet I don't know. We didn't go for long because the water was low, and the boat kept striking rocks."

Again, we can't help but notice the innocence of Reba as a 16-year-old, unsure if riding in a boat with boys was "proper".

Though she speaks about school she says very little about any of her classes. She does mention Latin and French.

On another day, she says, "After 4, Carrie and I went for our music lessons." No doubt this explains the two certificates from the Canadian College of Music that I found in her papers. The first certifies that Reba Ethel Hern had been awarded this first-class certificate of merit for piano playing. The second certificate specifies that she had received honours for piano playing. Her music teacher's name is given and the date is June 30th, 1928. This suggests that she had achieved a level of proficiency in playing. This was no doubt an advantage in her years of ministry.

As mentioned, her journal suggests that the predominant activities of the sisters revolved around the church. A typical Sunday included morning service at 11 a.m., Sunday School at 2:00 p.m., and evening service at 7:00 p.m.

This seems to have taken place in different churches. She speaks of Central Methodist Church, St. Andrews Presbyterian, and St. John's Methodist, all located in Sault Ste. Marie.

What she does not comment on was the importance of 1925 as the year in which the Methodist Church, the Presbyterian Church, and the Congregational Church all merged together to form "The United Church of Canada". At sixteen years of age, was she fully aware of the significance of that action? This merger would prove to be of great importance in the lives of the two sisters, but at age 16, she was probably not too interested in the happenings in the larger denominational world.

"On Sunday morning, Carrie and I went to church at John Street to hear Mr. Jeffries' last sermon. He is very bitter about leaving. Mama and Aunt Minnie went to St. Andrews Presbyterian Church. In the evening, we all went to Central Methodist Church for the inauguration service of the union church."

At this same time, we also hear of Rev. Smith leaving Central. His final sermon "was a twenty-minute lecture on the beauties of nature, and he said very little about leaving."

Soon we hear of Reverend Andrews preaching for the first time.

Further evidence of the changes is evident as Reba reports: "In the evening we went to St. Andrews, formerly Presbyterian. Mr. Pritchard from Toronto preached a fairly good sermon. The music however wasn't much." (Already we begin to see Reba's discernment about the quality of the music and the messages in the various services.)

It would appear that these church activities were those of the females in the family. She doesn't mention her dad going to church or Sunday School. From things that Reba said later, I doubt that Uncle Herb was a regular in church attendance, if he attended at all.

At another point during that year, she relates that a Miss Duff, a great temperance worker from Toronto, was in the city and was going to speak at a meeting at the church.

"Hers was just an ordinary lengthy talk on the temperance question. She tried to form a Young Women's Christian Temperance Union."

It is worth turning aside from Reba's journal to investigate the background of the Women's Temperance Movement and its relation to Prohibition.

"The Woman's Christian Temperance Union (WCTU)[11] was the largest non-denominational women's organization in 19th century Canada. Believing that alcohol abuse was the cause of unemployment, disease, sex work, poverty, violence against women and children, and immorality, the WCTU campaigned for the legal prohibition of all alcoholic beverages. Its membership was drawn from Canada's growing middle class, and its members held evangelical Protestant views. The WCTU also advocated for women's suffrage in Canada as a way to effect legislative change towards prohibition."

Reba remarks, "As most of us had so many organizations already, we did not want one and it wasn't organized."

Family life in the Hern household at that time was complicated by the presence of the girls' grandparents. It becomes obvious from her notes that her maternal grandparents, Grandma and Grandpa Stinson were both in ill health and had come to live with their daughter, Carrie. I am sure that their presence in the home was a learning experience for the girls as it would certainly affect the whole family.

Months of Grandpa's illness followed, culminating in his death.

"Carrie and I were called into the bedroom. We came up and stood at the foot of the bed." (The twins were 17 years of age).

"In awe, we gazed at Grandpa as he was passing from this world into the other. Grandma was kneeling by the bed with her head very close to his. He whispered in Grandma's ear, 'Jesus is mine.' His was indeed a lovely death."

Without doubt this experience was a wonderful preparation for the day when she would, as a minister, share with families in their loss of loved ones. In fact, her whole life would be influenced by these early experiences.

There followed the preparations for a funeral from the home, as was the case before funeral homes became popular.

It is interesting that no minister came, but instead a man who had known Grandpa. He was very old but a very fine man and he read scripture. In a quiet but strong voice, he read from the King James Bible. Listen with your heart to some of the words of these famous passages.

---

11   www.theCanadianencyclopedia.ca/enarticle/
     Womans-christian-temperance-union

Psalm 121: "I will lift up mine eyes unto the hills, from whence cometh my help. My help cometh from the LORD, which made heaven and earth. He will not suffer thy foot to be moved: he that keepeth thee will not slumber. Behold, he that keepeth Israel shall neither slumber nor sleep. The LORD is thy keeper: the LORD is thy shade upon thy right hand. The sun shall not smite thee by day, nor the moon by night. The LORD shall preserve thee from all evil: he shall preserve thy soul. The LORD shall preserve thy going out and thy coming in from this time forth, and even for evermore."

He also read from Isaiah 55:1 and from Revelation 22:13-14: "I am Alpha and Omega, the beginning and the end, the first and the last. Blessed are they that do his commandments, that they may have right to the tree of life, and may enter in through the gates into the city."

"We all knelt and he prayed which was very nice."

The funeral was conducted from the home as was customary when the body was laid out in the home and at the graveside.

As we have reviewed the life of a youthful Reba, we recognize that all of this lays the foundation for her own later experience as a minister and as a teacher of Religious Knowledge at Government High School in Nassau as we will hear about in future chapters.

Chapter Five

Preparing for Ministry

"Experience is a good teacher - but the tuition is high"

—Author unknown

When we last left her as a 16-year-old in Sault St. Marie, I asked myself, so how did a 16-year-old girl in 1925 receive a call to study for the ministry at a time when it was not at all an expected or even an acceptable profession for a woman? Or how did her sister come to marry a man who also decided to study for the ministry? Of this we have no record.

There are no journals to cover the years from 1925 to 1957.

How I wish that Reba had continued on with her practice of writing about her day-by-day activities. That leaves a period of 32 years of silence. It is possible, of course, that she did keep a diary during these years, but if so, we do not have them.

But we are not left entirely in the dark. In 1956, after Reba had left the ministry, and spent time in a convent, she worked for the Catholic Children's Aid Society (a story in itself which we shall explore later) and filled out a statement of her work experience.

In this statement, she indicates that she graduated from Collegiate Institute, Sault Ste. Marie, Ontario in 1927. Like many other young women, she worked as a waitress for at least one summer in Muskoka, north of Toronto to help pay for school. By 1931, or '32 she was heading to Toronto to study for her B.A. degree, followed by ministry training.

One might easily forget that these years were at the very heart of the Great Depression.

"Beginning on Black Tuesday, October 29, 1929, when the value of the New York stock market fell dramatically, and ending in 1939, the Great Depression was a time when Canadians suffered unprecedented levels of poverty due to unemployment. The unemployment rate was approximately 30 per cent and one in five Canadians depended on government relief for survival."[12]

As I consider this, I wonder how Reba had sufficient funds to attend Victoria College, followed by Emmanuel College from 1931-1937. How much did her father financially contribute to the higher education of Reba and her twin sister Carrie? I don't know the answer to that question. Without doubt he had the ability to pay her way. Unlike so many who were suffering unemployment through these years, Uncle Herb (Reba's father) was steadily employed as a millwright at the Pulp Mill in Sault Ste. Marie.

Again, in spite of her early involvement in the life of the United Church as a young woman, one is left to wonder where the incentive came from to enroll in a theological College. In later years, she indicated that it was her mother's idea, but I doubt that this is a satisfactory answer.

It is possible that she might have heard about Lydia Gruchy[13], a young woman "who emigrated to Canada from France with other family members into pioneer life in rural Saskatchewan. Lydia took up her dead brother's call to mission among the waves of poor immigrants arriving on the prairies."

As stated by Patricia Wotton, "Hers is a woman's story, set against the background of the suffragette movement and the wave of independent women leaders following World War I. No less than Nellie McClung[14] became involved in this new struggle.

"Lydia completed her first-class teaching certificate in 1918 and went on to teach in one room school houses. In this way she was able to support herself through studies at the University of Saskatchewan."

---

12 https://www.history/museum.ca/cmc/exhibitions/hist/mesicare/medic-2c01s. html

13 Patricia Wotton, *With Love, Lydia: the Story of Canada's First Woman Ordained Minister* (e-book, 2012), p. vii.

14 A Canadian women's suffragist and temperance advocate, Nellie McClung was one of the "Famous Five" Alberta women who initiated and won the Persons Case to have women recognized as persons under the BNA Act. https://www. thoughtco.com/nellie-mcclung-

"In 1920, she graduated with a Bachelor of Arts degree plus the Governor General's Gold Medal for academic excellence and leadership."[15]

In that same year, she received a scholarship from the Presbyterian Theological College for two years of study. "For the first time in the history of Canada, a woman will enter upon the regular course of theological training."[16] Dr. Oliver, the Principal of the College was convinced that ordination for women was imminent. Says Lydia, "I wasn't interested in ordination. I said as long as the work is with children, I'd like to do it, but I will never stand in front of adults and preach." Yet she did it.

Working at first as a teacher of immigrant children, with Sunday worship in the local schoolhouse or in an uninsulated church building left unheated through the week days, Lydia travelled 20 or 30 miles on horseback on a Sunday circuit of her pastoral charge.

Regular Sunday worship services soon led to a demand for more ministerial services. Funerals were possible, but baptism, quarterly communion, and weddings required an ordained minister. For each occasion, Lydia would arrange with a neighbouring ordained minister to travel to her small churches. It was not long before the ministers of Kamsack Presbytery began to ask themselves, "Why can't Lydia just do it?"

Writing in 1975, Lydia says, "The late Edmund H. Oliver, then principal of the Presbyterian Theological College, Saskatoon, had been instrumental in my taking theology. When the type of Home Mission charge to which I was appointed came to involve the whole range of pastoral work, it was he who championed the cause of my ordination. And hence, the ordination of women."

But many were opposed. "She cannot be ordained. The brethren won't stand for it."[17] The article, though, continues, "The movement is growing: 367 women are students in regular standing at theological colleges throughout the Dominion." This would seem to indicate that there was a movement taking place among women, far beyond the confines of Reba's world of which she may not even have been aware. In light of the fact that Reba was the first

---

15 Wotton, *With Love, Lydia*, p. 42.

16 Ibid. p. 47.

17 Wotton, *With love, Lydia*, p. 61.

woman to graduate from Emmanuel, I wonder where all these other women were enrolled?

As I said, I have no idea if Reba had ever heard of Lydia. The above article was written in 1923, when she was still 14 years old. Of course, the question of ordination at that time was on the back burner because of the negotiations between the Presbyterian Church, the Methodist Church, and the Congregational Church. Their merger into the United Church of Canada took place in 1925.

The ten-year struggle for ordination was not carried on by Lydia, but by others on her behalf. At last, "at the General Council Meeting of 1936, the remit results were affirmed by vote.... The vote for the ordination of women was carried by a landslide vote of the men of the church."

As interesting as Lydia's story is, it was happening in Saskatchewan, far away from Sault Ste. Marie and I doubt very much that Reba was familiar with Lydia's case until she enrolled in College.

Whatever the degree of her knowledge of precedents, Reba first enrolled in Victoria College where she proceeded to study for her B.A. degree in 1931, or 1932. She graduated in 1934.

Let's look at the background of that school and its successor.

The Methodists founded the Upper Canada Academy in 1836. In 1841 it became Victoria College, later Victoria University, part of the University of Toronto.

In an article entitled "Celebrating 121 Years! - Victoria University" we learn more about the status of women in the late 19th and early 20th centuries.[18]

"If we look back at some of the achievements of the VWA, we cannot emphasize enough the extraordinary impact this Association has had on the education of women, particularly in the early years when it was especially difficult for women to pursue higher education."

In the nineteenth century, women were not fully integrated into Canadian society, let alone the academic world. Consider there were men and also women who believed university education for women was unnecessary and possibly threatening to the social structure. Remember also, women did not get the vote in Canada until 1919, nor were they declared persons until 1929.

---

18   "Celebrating 121 Years! – Victoria University" University of Toronto, http://www.vicu.utotonto.ca/alumni/vwa/120.htm

"Cognizant of all the challenges that faced women, the Association actively encouraged them to attend university, aided them financially whenever possible, and, in 1903, provided them with a 'convenient and comfortable home.'"

Emmanuel College grew out of Union College, the successor of Knox College, the Presbyterian school for educating its clergy. Following the formation of the United Church of Canada in 1925, Union College united with the Faculty of Theology of Victoria College. The new college took the name "Emmanuel" in 1928, from the words under the figure of John Wesley in stained glass in the Victoria College Chapel: "The best of all is, God is with us." Emmanuel became 'an organ by which the Church trains its young men for the ministry and promotes theological learning.' It was in this College that Reba enrolled and from which she graduated in 1937.

I am interested to discover in *A History of Emmanuel College - The Toronto Years: 1930-1945* that the one entry for 1937 is: "Reba E. Hern becomes the first woman to receive a diploma from Emmanuel College."[19]

I suspect that it may have been here in Emmanuel, that Reba first learned of Lydia, since I am sure the College would be abuzz with the word of this strong woman in Saskatchewan who was being considered as a candidate for ordination.

Apart from all of that, I ask the question, "Was she happy with what she was taught at Emmanuel College?"

This is a serious question because I have every reason to believe that Reba came to Emmanuel as a genuine believer in the Lord Jesus and in the infallibility of God's Word. It must have been quite a shock to her to enter an environment where everything she had taken for granted was being questioned.

Writing much later, in 1965, in a notebook she called "My Social Life," she writes of her feelings of what was taught in Emmanuel. Perhaps this was not what she thought at the time but after years of reflection, she felt that what she was taught was that:

"What is against my interests is evil and the theories and moral standards that please me are right. I am the standard of truth, not the Word of God."

She says, "All through my whole theological studies there was this degrading of God and the exalting of man. The professors all felt this to be

---

19   http://www.vivu.utoronto.ca/sbout/History _of Victoria/1930-1945.htm

a wonderful step forward in our religious life and I can't think of a single student but myself who wasn't deeply influenced by them.

"Original sin was quite passé. In fact, sin on the whole was not sin, but some kind of illness. A physical thing but not a spiritual one. To believe in the devil, you were a little odd. He most certainly no longer existed. How smug they all were! Mankind and the world could only go up and up. We had reached a new day of liberty and fullness.

"But all this was false. No matter whether we believe in a devil or not, we can't change facts and the truth is, he is a fact of life, and the fact of evil in the world is there regardless of all. And now I can look back over the years and see the result of all this."

When we consider the time period, between the disastrous First World War, followed by the Great Depression, and the horrendous terrors of the Second World War, it is hard to believe that those training for ministry would consider that "mankind can only go up and up"

Certainly, this teaching was far removed from the card signed by an eleven-year-old girl, which I showed in Chapter Three.

There was good reason for Reba's concerns about what she learned in Emmanuel College. What she was learning was the outgrowth of the liberalism and the Higher Criticism, which had been influencing theological education in America since the middle of the 19th century.

In a lengthy but excellent article by Canon Dyson Hague, [20] well worthy of our attention, he explains that Higher Criticism was based upon, "attacks upon the Bible and the supernatural character of the Holy Scriptures. In the first place, the critics who were the leaders... have been men who have based their theories largely upon their own subjective conclusions."

He makes it clear that the dominant men of the movement were men with a strong bias against the supernatural. Some of the men who have been most distinguished as the leaders of the Higher Critical movement in Germany and Holland have been men who have no faith in the God of the Bible, and

---

20 "The History of the Higher Criticism," R.A. Torry and Canon Dyson Hague, Rector of the Memorial Church, London, Ontario. Lecturer in Liturgics and Ecclesiology, Wycliffe College, Toronto, Canada. Examining Chaplain to the Bishop of Huron.
    https://www.blueletterbible.org/Comm/torrey_ra/fundamentals/01.cfm

no faith in either the necessity or the possibility of a personal supernatural revelation and have been notoriously opposed to the miraculous.

When I myself was in seminary, I too had to study the teachings of the higher critics. Just like the teaching of evolution, I found it took far more faith to believe these theories than it took to believe the Bible. I have never understood how false teaching in any of these fields could capture the minds of professors, students, and ultimately the people in the churches.

There is something in the rebellious human spirit, which prefers teaching which discredits the scriptures and seeks to throw doubt upon their authority.

Canon Hague says that these "were men who had discarded belief in God and Jesus Christ Whom He had sent. The Bible, in their view, was a mere human product. It was a stage in the literary evolution of a religious people." The result of these teachings, says Canon Hague, is "a discredited Pentateuch, a discredited Old Testament, and a discredited Bible. But its most serious feature is this: It is a theory of inspiration that completely overturns the old-fashioned ideas of the Bible and its unquestioned standard of authority and truth."

This was the teaching that had gripped Emmanuel College and other seminaries long before Reba arrived on the scene.

In contrast to the foundational doctrines of the Anglican, the Presbyterian, the Methodist, and other churches, which were all based upon the view that the Bible contains the truth, the whole truth, and nothing but the truth, these new teachings doubted the word of Christ Jesus our Lord who believed and emphatically affirmed the Mosaic authorship of the Pentateuch. This he made clear in Matthew 5:17-18; Mark 12:26-36; Luke 16:31; John 5:46-47, and many other scriptures but these were all explained away.

"The critics say that either, "Christ knew the views He taught were false, and yet taught them as truth, or else, Christ didn't know they were false and believed them to be true when they were not true. In either case the Blessed One is dethroned as "True God and True Man"

This is the teaching that had swept across the United States and Canada during the late 19th century and the early 20th century.

Says L.K. Tarr [21] of the Fellowship of Evangelical Baptist Churches in Canada, "The division of the 1920's took place during the decade in which the modernist-Fundamentalist controversy raged at its height in the United States. That struggle convulsed several Protestant denominations and issued in the emergence of new Evangelical groupings. The divisions did not immediately occur for the Evangelicals frequently won the initial skirmishes. Gradually, however, the liberals or modernists succeeded in wresting control of several major theological seminaries and the denominational machinery. The Evangelicals or Fundamentalists were either expelled or withdrew from the original denominations."

Such was the case in the Baptist Convention of Ontario and Quebec, the culmination of a struggle, which had begun before 1910. The denominational school, McMaster University, hired two professors in succession, Dr. I.G. Matthews, followed by Professor L.H. Marshall, "a personable and outspoken liberal."

After years of controversy, in 1927, the Baptist Convention showed its acceptance of liberal theology by expelling Pastor Dr. T.T. Shields, Jarvis Street Baptist Church, and a number of other churches, resulting ultimately in The Fellowship of Evangelical Baptist Churches in Canada in which the present writer has been a pastor for 50 years.

Writing on the subject "Higher Criticism in Canada" Johan D. Tangelder[22] says, "Canada used to have a Christian moral consensus. Now it is living on Christian memories."

Ben Smillie, writing in the *United Church Observer* in 1967, is a good example, in my opinion, of the deceptive teachings which gripped many of these denominations. He states: "If Adam and Eve, Cain and Abel, Noah and Jonah are personages in myth and allegory, they cannot be historical people at the same time, no matter how sincere one's faith. Does somebody question this? Then look at the Bible documents. Any student who has done a basic course on the Bible knows since the days of Karl Graf and Julius Wellhausen

---

21 L.K. Tarr, *This Dominion, His Dominion: The story of the Evangelical Baptist Endeavour in Canada.* (Fellowship of Evangelical Churches in Canada, 1968), p. 69.

22 Reformed Reflections http://www.reformedreflections.ca/other-religions/uc-higher-criticism-in-ca.html

that the first six books of the Bible are composite literary works, containing myths, legends, law and priestly ritual."[23]

In this, he assumes that these men whom he regards as "two giants of Old Testament scholarship at the end of the nineteenth century" were reliable witnesses. Having spent my life in ministry, and having read the abundant scholars who find the Bible completely trustworthy, I consider the above statement by Ben Smillie and also held by the leadership of the United Church, to be completely untrue.

But these were the teachings to which Reba was exposed as a student in Emmanuel College. She was one student among many, the majority of whom would be men. Her professors were also men. Already she must have been experiencing what it was like to be a woman in what up to this time had been a man's world. I don't know to what degree she would be willing to stand out from her teachers and classmates to question these new ideas.

I think Reba was a true believer when she entered those hallowed halls and it appears that she must have found the viewpoints of some of her professors shocking and not according to her own beliefs. Her comments which I have quoted above might reflect a later cynicism, but they do suggest that she was not totally pleased with what she was learning in Seminary and was perhaps already experiencing some disillusionment. Certainly, this would lead, either to hiding her true beliefs or developing a strong character.

Were these liberal ideas widespread in the denomination? As always is the case, changes in theology take time to filter out to local churches. In our little country church, we first really were aware of the greatness of the shift in the introduction of the new curriculum in the sixties.

"The first curriculum developed entirely in Canada was the United Church's 'New Curriculum'[24] of 1963. It was attacked in the media by conservative denominations for being too 'liberal' in its theology and ended several decades of curriculum co-operation between the United and Baptist churches."

It was this curriculum which finally forced my mother and myself to seek out Biblical teaching, first in the Brethren, and then among the Fellowship

---

23   Ben Smillie, United Church Observer, 1967

24   Sunday Schools | The Canadian Encyclopedi
     https://www.thecanadianencyclopedia.ca/en/article/sunday-schools

Baptists. Though Reba and I would have been in agreement at this stage of her life, still it is true that we followed two different paths of religious thought as she struggled with some of the liberal viewpoints, while I followed the more traditional conservative outlook.

But while Reba may have been concerned by what she learned at Emmanuel, she nonetheless was learning – learning how to study, learning how to form independent opinions, and learning how to minister to others, which she would put into practice during her ministry years.

It was also the foundation which prepared her to teach Religious Knowledge in the Government High School in Nassau. She was a compassionate teacher and made a difference in the lives of her students.

Chapter Six

Almost There!

"Character may almost be called the most effective means of persuasion."

— Aristotle

Yes, Reba was learning. In fact, she was supposed to be ready to step out into a local church, which was unusual, because only one other woman, Lydia Gruchy, was in the United Church ministry. In the last chapter, I told her story and quoted from a newspaper article, written in 1923, which claimed that 367 women were in theological studies at that time, but did not explain where those women were studying.

This was definitely uncharted territory. Reba was going to need to develop a strong character if she was to survive in a heretofore man's world in the United Church.

Before she graduated from Emmanuel College, Reba was sent on a summer ministry experience to Saskatchewan. This was normal protocol for all aspiring preachers.

She received a Form Letter from the Board of Home Missions.

March 30, 1936

Miss Reba Hern

Dear Sir:

This is to notify you that you have been appointed as Student Missionary to serve in the Mission Field of Peebles, Sask. (5 congregations) in the Presbytery of Qu'Appelle.

(Here follows the names of the Superintendent of Missions, the Convener of Home Missions and her supervising Pastor. She is to write these men "telling them when they may expect you on your field.")

You will be expected to reach your field for Sunday April 26 and to remain until September 27. Your salary will be at the rate of $10.50 per week and board, plus cost of your transportation on the field up to approximately $30.00

Very sincerely yours,

R. B. Cochrane

Oh, wow! $10.50 plus board! It is also humorous to note that Mr. Cochrane is so used to sending letters only to male students that he mistakenly addresses her as "Dear Sir".

Can you imagine any ministry student, whether male or female, being assigned to five congregations? As a pastor myself, I have never faced a challenge of this degree. I rather think she would need guidance from her ministry supervisor to help her understand how to approach the task.

Lydia Gruchy could have told her from her own experience of the trials of this kind of pastoral ministry, because Lydia had been there, done that. Did Reba know Lydia's story? I suspect that as a student at Emmanuel, she had heard of her, since her reputation was probably well known in United Church circles by that time.

Was Reba excited to be somewhat near to Lydia, who was ministering at St. Andrew's United Church in Moose Jaw? I would love to know whether Reba met Lydia during those weeks. I hope that she did and had the opportunity to hear firsthand about the 13-year process leading to her upcoming ordination that November, after Reba would return to Toronto. At the very least, she would be aware of what was taking shape just a few miles away in Moose Jaw.

That summer Reba completed her student ministry assignment. She must have done all right because at the end of the summer she received another letter.

September 8, 1936

Miss Reba Hern

Windthorst, Sask.,

My dear Miss Hern,

I trust that you have been having an enjoyable summer and that you have felt your work has been abundantly worthwhile.

The General Council opens in Ottawa on September 23rd. Friday evening of that week is our Home Mission night, when we try to present in a series of brief addresses a bird's eye view of the United Church Home Mission activities across Canada. Mr. Beaton and I feel that it would be a unique and attractive feature if you, as our only woman student missionary, could be present to speak for ten minutes about your experience this summer. This would mean that you would have to leave about the 21st of September, but under the circumstances, we think you ought to be able to arrange to do so.

If you would be willing... wire me collect, so that we could send you your transportation direct to Ottawa. Of course, we will look after all the expenses of your stay there.

... It might be helpful for both you and ourselves if you could take time to write out what you are going to say and give us a chance to go over it with you in advance. We might be able to make some suggestions, which would be worthwhile.

Very sincerely yours,

R.B. Cochrane.

In this letter, I note that Mr. Cochrane addressed her personally and properly as Miss Hern, and not Sir as in the former form letter.

Reba returned from the west that summer, and no doubt gave an interesting account of the challenges of trying to minister to five congregations. I suspect that male student ministers did the same.

In November, Lydia was ordained. The story of her ordination is given in her biography, *With Love, Lydia*, which confirms that Miss Gruchy was not only the first woman ordained in the United Church of Canada but the first woman ordained in any denomination in Canada.

Thus, in western Canada, one woman had opened the door to ordination for other women across the country.

Lydia's biographer, Pat Wotton says that, "The question most asked of her was how she was received as a woman in ministry, or as more commonly called, 'a Lady Minister'? Rev. Gruchy's reply was consistently, "I can see no difference in whether a minister is male or female. I have always been invited to any charge I've taken and found the congregation in the main, are not opposed to seeing a woman in the pulpit."[25]

"On the subject of 'Lady Ministers' Lydia Gruchy had one other observation to offer. 'All other things being equal...you will still find today, that a man will be called to the pulpit before a woman.' Then, eyes twinkling she added: 'After all, a woman's better than nothing.'"

Meanwhile, things were moving forward in Reba's life.

In the spring of 1937, Reba graduated from Emmanuel College, Toronto.

In a letter dated May 6th, 1937, Charles D. Donald, Chairman, Algoma Presbytery, Toronto Conference of the United Church of Canada writes:

> "This is to certify that Miss Reba Hern, B.A., a graduate in theology of Emmanuel College, Victoria University, and a student for the ministry under the care of this Presbytery, has this day, after due examination, been duly licensed to preach the Gospel wherever she may be orderly called or appointed and is hereby commended to the Toronto Conference for ordination to the Christian ministry of the word and sacraments."
>
> Charles D. Donald Chairman, R.E. Gorse, secretary,
>
> John St., Church, Sault Ste. Marie, Ont.

25 Wotton, *With Love, Lydia,* p. 178 and 179

Reba Hern Graduation picture – Emmanuel College 1937

In another article from *The New Outlook*, May 28, 1937:

"A Lady is Licensed to Preach"

"Miss Reba Hern, B.A., a recent graduate of Emmanuel College, Toronto, was licensed to preach at a meeting of the Algoma Presbytery, held on May 6, in John St. United Church, Sault Ste. Marie, Ontario where Miss Hern is a member.... After the ceremony, the ladies of the congregation held a reception and presented the new licentiate with a basket of flowers, and on behalf of the Algoma Presbytery presented her with a loose-leaf Bible. Since this was the first occasion that a service of this kind has been conducted by the Presbytery, and since Miss Hern is the first woman to be licensed in Eastern Canada, the event is historic. Miss Hern is recommended to the Toronto Conference for ordination at its next meeting."

Reba Hern - Graduation certificate

From the United Church of Canada Archives:[26]

> "Miss Hern is listed on the candidates' Ordained list of the United Church of Canada Yearbook of 1937, meaning that she was ordained in only the second year that women were able to be ordained. Reba Hern was indeed the second (woman) ordained in 1938."

On the occasion of her ordination, Reba was presented with a beautifully inscribed Minister's Record Book in which to record sermons preached, members received on profession of faith, marriages, baptisms and funerals.

---

26 Letter from Robin Brunelle, Reference Assistant, United Church of Canada Archives, received March 3, 2009

The inscription: "Presented to the Rev. Reba Ethel Hern, B.A. on the occasion of her ordination into the ministry of the United Church of Canada by the members and friends of John St. United Church of Canada, Sault Ste. Marie, Ont. June 20, 1937." They then included the following verse, Galatians 6:9: "And let us not be weary in well doing: for in due season we shall reap, if we faint not." Along with her journals, I have that Record Book. I value it highly.

Truly, this was historic. Like Lydia Gruchy in Saskatchewan, Reba was breaking new ground in Ontario. Regardless of the future, she was ordained and ready to step into the pulpit.

At the ordination of Mary Hallett in 1986, Lydia told an interesting story quoted by her biographer, Patricia Wotton: "The twinkle comes again to her eye as she tells us that the second woman to be ordained was from Toronto. 'You'll appreciate this as westerners,' she says. 'I have had people say to me, "I was at your ordination." "Oh, were you at Moose Jaw?" "No, in Toronto." They just assume that the first woman ordained in Toronto had to be the first in Canada.' The Reverend Reba Hern was ordained in Toronto, two years later in 1938."[27]

So, she had achieved her dream - or had she?

She has left no record of the kind of difficulties experienced by Lydia, but are we to suppose that such problems would not be experienced by Reba Hern? I have long suspected that the reason Reba left the ministry after two pastorates was due to the fact that she was a woman in an old boys' club who may or may not have been helped in that difficult experience by her minister brother-in-law.

Lydia's biographer says, "Perhaps more pertinently, she knew better than anyone, how demanding life in the ministry was…she well recognized that ready acceptance of women in the pulpit would be a long time coming. For any woman minister, positive acknowledgement would be grudging, slow and in some cases, refused. A serious candidate for the ordained ministry would have to be determined and certain of her calling."

A humorous statement, though, may be applicable at this point in the story. This was quoted by Miss Gruchy: "I told them…how I felt like I was being treated like a weed in a rose garden…I knew I was not a weed, and I

---

27 Wotton, *With Love, Lydia*, p. 157

wasn't sure that they were all roses."[28] Perhaps Reba could have said 'Amen' to that tongue-in-cheek comment.

We have no record of how Reba felt about her ordination at that time, but the ministry proved to be a mixed blessing. There must be some reason why she resigned her ministry after only 13 years.

So, how will this all play out when she actually steps into the pulpit and begins the work for which she had been trained? We'll find out as we look forward to "Her Ministry Years."

---

28   Quoted from "Her Story" http://library.usask.ca/herstory/gruchy.html

CHAPTER SEVEN

Her Ministry Years

"A man could retire nicely in his old age if he could sell his experience for what it cost him.

— Author unknown

I am sure that Reba must have been excited to finally be finished with Emmanuel College, and ready to plunge into the actual work for which she had been trained.

Her ministry began right in her home area, on July 4, 1937, just a couple of months after her graduation. It was a four-point charge, typical of ministry in rural Canada in those years but certainly not an easy assignment.

She found herself responsible for four small country churches in Rydal Bank, Dunn's Valley, Rock Lake and Poplar Dale, and later Cloudslee, all no more than 40 miles from Sault Ste. Marie where she had grown up. She was serving in the same presbytery which had ordained her in John Street United Church. These rural communities lay to the north of Bruce Mines, Ontario. Reba would live in the parsonage at Rydal Bank and would have to travel to each of these churches every Sunday.

Although she preached the same sermon four times each Sunday, this would be a very demanding schedule. My brother, Gordon, reports that she drove a 1938 Ford Coupe in the summer and drove a horse and cutter in the winter. She must have been an excellent horsewoman because Gordon says that she visited the farm once with a very high-spirited "driver" and cutter and when she left, it was in a great haste. It rather reminds me of the ministers coming to the church that I attended as a boy. A four-point charge required the minister to always be in a hurry, which led us to refer to him as the "sky pilot".

How I wish that Reba had left a written record of her impressions of these years of ministry.

What I do have, though, is a record of the sermons she preached in those four churches. These are found in "The Minister's Record" book, which was presented to her at her ordination as mentioned above. Even a casual glance thrills me as a Pastor.

Her titles are delightful.

Her first sermon was "We would see Jesus" from John 12:21. The story tells of certain Gentiles who came to Philip and requested, "Sir, we would see Jesus." On the basis of this request, Jesus saw the evidence that, "The hour has come that the Son of Man should be glorified," thus predicting his death. I wish that I had been in the audience that day to have heard that first message, but I was not born for another two years.

Sunday by Sunday the sermons poured forth. "God's Jewel Case" from Ephesians 1:1-23; "Broken Cisterns" from Jeremiah 2:1-13; "The Price of Souls". This was taken from John 12:24: "Most assuredly, I say to you, unless a grain of wheat falls into the ground and dies, it remains alone; but if it dies, it produces much grain." Following on from John 12:21, Jesus clearly indicated that he was well aware that the grain of wheat which falls into the ground and dies referred to himself. This was the price of souls. It was the way in which he could produce abundant fruit.

Can you not get a picture of this young 28-year-old woman speaking to the hearts of her farmer hearers?

"Our Every Care", 1 Peter 5:9; "An Instrument of Ten Strings", Psalm 144:9; "The Making of a Hero", Judges 3:7 – 9; "Almost Persuaded"; "God's Landmarks", Acts 16:31; "Charge That To My Account", Philemon verses 17, 18.

The messages continue: "The Tree That Never Dies" comes from Psalm 1. "Blessed is the man Who walks not in the counsel of the ungodly, Nor stands in the path of sinners, Nor sits in the seat of the scornful; But his delight is in the law of the LORD, And in His law he meditates day and night. He shall be like a tree planted by the rivers of water, that brings forth its fruit in its season, whose leaf also shall not wither; And whatever he does shall prosper."

Not only are her sermon titles beautifully descriptive, but her wide range of biblical passages is also telling. In her first year of ministry she preached from John's Gospel, from Ephesians, from Exodus, Numbers, Jeremiah, Genesis, Philippians, 1 Peter, Psalms, 1 Samuel, Luke, 1 Corinthians, 2 Peter, Acts, Galatians, Judges, Daniel.

In her second year, she included Revelation, and again a wide selection. What this tells me is that Reba was reading widely from her whole Bible and finding real profit from doing so. Just viewing her sermon titles tells me that at that point Reba was not following the liberal views of her professors but was preaching a strong evangelical message.

Listen again to "The Greatest Moment of Jesus' Life;" "The Solitary Throne", John 14: 6; "As a Flame of Fire"; "The Hinterland of the Soul".

And listen to this one: "Photophobia": Do you know where that one came from? It was taken from John 3:19. "And this is the condemnation, that the light has come into the world, and men loved darkness rather than light, because their deeds were evil." It would appear that Reba had a genius for finding interesting titles for her messages.

On and on these great titles go:

"Life in a Look"; "Stepping Stones Toward Peace"; "Which Road Shall I Take?"

I wish I could have been there to hear that vibrant young woman preaching messages such as these. You wouldn't go to sleep under that preaching the way the farmers used to go to sleep in the 3 p.m. services in Alma Heights United where us single fellows hunkered down in the back pew behind some lady's large hat and dozed off.

No, these were gripping sermons aimed at the heart. While visiting in the Bruce Mines area many years ago, I met Hugh Colver, who told me that he had been converted to faith in Christ under Reba Hern's preaching in one of these country churches.

At the same time, I doubt that her sermons pleased everyone. True preachers do not simply give nice stories to tickle the ear, nor do they parrot public opinion. Truth wounds the conscience, and a wounded conscience tends to make a person critical of the one who is stirring up memories one prefers to keep well buried. I have been forever thankful for a man who told me the truth in spite of the fact that the truth troubled my soul. It, at last, drove me to the Saviour who gave His life for me; I will spend eternity praising Him for His love and mercy.

Good preachers have always led people to say, "Who told him about me?" because the Bible has exposed areas of their lives which they did not want brought to the light.

I suspect that her preaching at that time led people to say, "If the Bible is true, she is telling me the truth for I can see it for myself." That was my experience as a young person sitting under a different preacher, who also gave me the clear teaching of God's Word.

This kind of preaching was not necessarily done by her fellow ministers, even those whom she had heard as a sixteen-year-old. You remember, for instance, the minister whose final message to his congregation was a twenty-minute lecture on the beauties of nature (Chapter Four). Of what value was that to the souls of the people in the pews that day?

Wedding of Wilbur and Carrie Rogers, Reba's sister

Reba remained in this northern area just four years, from September 1937 to June 1941. During this time, she preached more than 530 times, baptized 52 people, including 1 adult, received 30 people into membership on profession of their faith, and married 14 couples. I find it extremely interesting that one of those couples was her sister Carrie, who married Wilbur Rogers in Sault Ste. Marie on December 25, 1940. During those years she also conducted 30 funerals.

It should be noted that the last two years in the Rydal Bank charge and the first four years in Varna were war years. During that time, her cousin Alan Keith, a pilot flying out of Malta, was listed as missing in action. It might be asked what effect all of this had on her life as a minister.

I value a letter Alan wrote to her during that time, just before he failed to return from a mission and was presumed dead.

He wrote: "Dear Reba,

"I received your letter several weeks ago. I'm kind of slow at writing – there's not much to write about for one thing....

"I seem to be spending most of my time in hospital. I was in for six weeks with malaria soon after I arrived, and now I'm in again, with a few burns on my hand as the result of a forced landing..."

Shortly thereafter it is assumed that his plane went down, taking his life. He also wrote a letter to his father sharing his faith in Christ with his unbelieving dad. Many years later, when Uncle Lionel died, that letter was found in his drawer. I am sure that that witness prepared the way for Uncle Lionel's acceptance of the Lord before he passed away.

It should also be noted that during the war years a great many women were brought into the work force which was the beginning of a huge cultural shift. It did not stop there: the post-war period gave birth to modern feminism when women were expected to give up their jobs as the men returned.

All of this no doubt influenced Reba's life and ministry.

In July, 1941, she accepted a call to the Varna Pastoral Charge, which seems to have been another very rural area, this time in Huron County, not far from Lake Huron 30 miles south of Goderich. A look at a map shows Varna located just at a crossroad in a farming area.

Here, she served a three-point charge including Varna, Goshen, and Blake.

These were obviously small country churches but once again I notice sermon titles such as "Power for Service", Acts 1:8.

Within a month in her new charge, Reba preached on "The Greatest Moments of Jesus' Life". One might wonder what this young woman in a new pastorate would preach as the greatest moments of Jesus' life.

Her text was taken from 2 Corinthians 5:18-21: "Now all things are of God, who has reconciled us to Himself through Jesus Christ, and has given us the ministry of reconciliation, that is, that God was in Christ reconciling the world to Himself, not imputing their trespasses to them, and has committed to us the word of reconciliation. Now then, we are ambassadors for Christ, as though God were pleading through us: we implore you on Christ's behalf, be reconciled to God. For He made Him who knew no sin to be sin for us, that we might become the righteousness of God in Him."

It was this last verse which speaks of Christ's atoning sacrifice on the cross, taking our sin upon Himself, being literally "made sin for us, so that we might be made righteous" that she gives as the greatest achievement of Christ's life on earth. Here was the birth and the foundation of the church, raised up as God's agent of reconciliation for the world. Here is clear evidence that Reba was no mouther of platitudes, but a true preacher of the gospel.

Her message titles continue: "The Heavenly Porter," "The Struggle of Prayer," "Let the Fire Fall" and "The World's Strangest Prayer Room" (this one about Jonah praying in the belly of the whale). Some messages carry the same titles as those in her former charge.

Listen once more: "Broken Cisterns"; "There Stood a Man"; "Second Chance"; "God's Jewel Case"; God's Autograph Album." No doubt, those sermons which she had delivered in her first pastorate would be expanded and deepened in her second ministry.

We need to keep these so obviously Christ-centered, Spirit-filled messages in mind as we follow the immense changes which took place in the years which followed.

In my research, I had the good fortune to be in touch with Reverend Colin Snyder, a United Church minister now serving (2017) at Trinity United Church, Listowel, Ontario. Colin actually pastored in the same churches in which Reba served.

In response to my request for information about her, Rev. Snyder sent the following announcement to Brucefield Community United Church, which was created by the 2013 amalgamation of Brucefield, Kippen, Varna, and Goshen churches, asking that it be included in the Sunday bulletin, which is also posted on their Facebook page each week. The response has been encouraging.

Researching on my behalf, Colin sent to me a number of items received from people who were former parishioners. These reveal something of Reba's success as the minister of this three-point charge.

Says Rev. Snyder: "Her life is an important part of our United Church history and of this congregation."

In a hand-written letter, one of Reba's parishioners expresses the feelings of the congregation for their new minister. This may have been a report to the local newspaper.

"May, 1942

Young Woman Pastor Serves Huron Co. Church with Success

"Minister of Varna United Church, Rev. Reba Hern is the only ordained woman engaged in pastoral work in Canada at the present time.

"This slender, attractive young woman, still in her twenties, who dislikes a gown and appears in the pulpit in a plain dark dress or sometimes in summer in all-white, has attracted wide attention as a preacher.

"Any question as to the success of women in the ministry, and there are still questions in many conservative minds, seem answered by Miss Hern who takes three services each Sunday, in all weather, keeps in close touch with all her congregation and all her pastoral duties and lives by herself in the Varna parsonage where she has the advantage of the bachelor clergy in being able to cook her own meals, and where she also sturdily tends the big lawn surrounding the house.

"Unlike some of her masculine contemporaries, she does not read her sermons. Nor does she take notes into the pulpit.

"Her warm contralto voice carries well in any building and in the ten months of her ministry here, she has preached in

26 different pulpits and in some of these, as often as three different times.

"Rev. Reba Hern takes 3 services each Sunday and is in demand as a guest preacher."

Having never seen her in the pulpit, I am thankful for this word picture, which describes my cousin at that stage of her life although she was mistaken about Reba's age. The same writer writes of Reba's reception in the presbytery and how she dealt with the matter of being a woman in the pulpit. It is obvious that she was comfortable in her role and not intimidated by the inevitable questions that were thrown at her in those days before the presence of women in ministry was commonplace.

Another article was sent to me in rather unsteady handwriting. These may have been submitted to and printed in a local paper. It is obvious that they were for publication. This one deals with churches to whom a woman minister was not yet fully accepted.

In the Presbytery

"When the news of Rev. Reba Hern's appointment to Varna reached Huron Presbytery, the subject of women preachers was a lively topic at many a church meeting. When she exchanged pulpits, the query arises as to her reception in the church: Should she be introduced to the congregation as a missionary speaker? Should she be escorted to the pulpit? Should the service be opened for her? But when she arrived at the church, a slender, capable young woman, and is introduced to the elders, she takes her place without any uncertainty. The fact that she is a woman preacher gives her no concern whatever; it is the work that matters and she suffers from neither inferiority or a superiority complex. And the question asked by an anxious Huron County United Church woman, "Wouldn't a woman look terribly out of place at conference?" was answered by another woman, though not by Miss Hern Herself, "Well, perhaps no more so than a man preacher at a quilting bee."

Note added: "Ron was the first baby baptized by a woman preacher – Miss Hern. Jean was also baptized by Miss Hern."

For nine years she carried on her ministry in these three churches. What is not mentioned are the many hours of study, the time assisting teachers in the Sunday School, the Board meetings, the hours and days of visiting families in their homes, perhaps sometimes being invited to stay for supper. Also not mentioned is the loneliness of living alone in a 'manse' or 'parsonage'. When the writer says that she was in demand as a guest preacher, this would also involve many hours of special preparation, and many miles of travel to various churches. She was one busy woman.

In all of this we see further preparation for a life that was yet to come, and about which she yet knew nothing. She could never have visualized the young black faces raised to hers as she taught them the basics of Religious Knowledge.

Along the way, she led in the building of a new church building in Goshen and the renovation of the building in Varna.

Reverend Snyder writes: "It was in 1948 that the Goshen congregation built and moved into a new church building, meaning that she was the first minister to serve from that pulpit, and I was, sadly, the last. I find this to be an interesting connection."

Below is the annual report for 1948, which reveals something of Reba's success during those years.

United Church of Canada
Annual Report
Of Varna, Goshen, and Blake
For the year ending December 31, 1948
MINISTER: Rev. Reba E. Hern, B.A.
Recording Secretary: Mr. Richard Robinson.

Dear friends,

The year 1948 was one of much accomplishment with the Goshen and Varna congregations. On the 21st of June there was the laying of the cornerstone of the new Goshen church, then on the 12th of December the opening of that church.

Certainly 1948 will be a "Red letter" year for Goshen. How proud the Goshen people can be of their lovely little church!

As it sits upon the top of the hill, may it ever be a blessing and a beacon to all the country around for our Lord.

Varna too saw many changes. The basement was dug not without difficulty, and the main auditorium was re-plastered and re-modelled. We must leave the record of the reopening of that church for the year 1949.

May our Lord bless you all, each and every one of our three congregations. As the work has prospered materially, may it also prosper in every soul.

Sincerely,

Reba E. Hern

As mentioned in her 1948 report, the Varna Church building was also undergoing extensive renovations. Below is its invitation to its re-opening.

You are invited to the re-opening
of the
Varna United Church
On Sunday the fifth of June
Nineteen hundred and forty-nine.
Services will be held at
11 a.m. and 7:30 p.m.
Special Speaker: Rev. E. A. Poulter
Soloists: Miss Mimi Johnston, Hamilton,
Granddaughter of Rev. D. Johnston, a former minister:
Mr. Don Hughes, Exeter,
Sherlock Keyes, Clerk of Session;   Reba E. Hern, Pastor

Perhaps the fact that the war had come to an end and a new era of prosperity had arrived may have spurred on the churches to new endeavours.

While Reba was busy preaching messages in Varna, Goshen, and Blake, her sister Carrie and brother-in-law Wilbur were also in the early stages of being brought into ministry life. Wilbur grew up on a farm near Bruce Mines, Ont. and became a member of the same John St. United Church in the Sault, from which Reba had been sent forth. It appears that Wilbur lived for a time in Saskatchewan so he too had a western connection. His records [29]indicate that he attended Avonlea High School, which must have been in Avonlea, Saskatchewan from 1926-29. He graduated from Regina College in 1932.

After five years Wilbur was received as a candidate for Queen's Theological College in Kingston, Ontario in September, 1937, the same year that Reba graduated from Emmanuel.

Graduating from Queen's College in 1942, he completed his ministerial studies in Emmanuel College from which he graduated in 1943, six years after Reba's ordination and two years after she moved to Varna. This would be of little interest to this story except for the fact that Wilbur's ministry was so closely related to Reba's and may have had an influence on her decision to leave the Church.

Wilbur's first ministry was also in his home area. From 1943 to 1945, Wilbur served as the minister in Little Rapids, Ontario (near Thessalon), 50 miles east of the Sault.

He next served in Dungannon, just north of Goderich, 1945-1948; and Blythe (just east of Goderich, and 30 miles north east of Varna) from 1948-1950. This was probably unfortunate because both of these pastorates were served during Reba's last five years in the nearby Varna-Goshen charge. For part of this time, Wilbur also served as Chairman of the Huron County Presbytery. In that capacity, he would have been Reba's direct superior. One might easily assume that Reba would be pleased to see her sister and brother-in-law (whom she had married) in ministry. Again, one would think that having her twin sister so close would have allowed them to spend many happy hours enjoying one another's company. It was during these years that Reba also baptized their oldest daughter Carol Ann.

But this is once more where speculation comes in because her journals clearly show that their relationship was often strained. I believe that serving alongside and then under the supervision of Wilbur might not have been

---

29 Survey form for the Archives of the United Church of Canada, filled out by Wilbur January 12, 1982

helpful. My knowledge of Wilbur, both from personal observation and Reba's diaries is that, unlike his sister-in-law, Wilbur was what I would call a "professional clergyman." Some may recognize that there is a difference.

During the nine years that Reba served the Varna charge, till April 23, 1950, she preached many sermons, baptized 56 children including her niece Carol Ann Rogers (May 30, 1943); received 41 into membership, married 19 couples, and conducted 33 funerals, including 25 between 1945 and 1950.

But here we find a curious thing. In her Minister's Record book, in which she had kept detailed and careful records of the sermons whose very titles have thrilled my soul, that record suddenly stopped November 25, 1945. Although she begins to once more keep track of her preaching from January 1949 to April 23, 1950, she no longer gave her sermon titles, but merely states that she preached in Varna, Goshen, and Blake. I cannot help but wonder why this change of practice for the last four and one-half years, even though she continued to record her other ministerial duties.

As we draw closer to the end of her active ministry, perhaps the record of messages disappeared because she was becoming stressed in her chosen occupation. Could it have been because she became completely dispirited during those last years? Yet, this change does not seem to accord with her evident success in leading in the construction of a new church building in Goshen and the renovation of the Varna building.

I believe that she must have found herself in a very difficult position - a woman in a traditional man's role. Although we have seen that she won her way within the churches under her leadership, I doubt that all of her male counterparts would have made it easy for her.

In 1966, Pierre Burton[30] 'at the behest of the Anglican Church' wrote *The Comfortable Pew.*[31]

Although he was critiquing the Anglican Church, "Berton offers a damning litany of complaint against the Protestant Church he saw in the '60s: which could equally apply to the established church as a whole."

In his book, *The Joy of Writing,* Mr. Berton states that, "It was the right moment for a critical review of the Church from a former layman and atheist.

---

30 Pierre, Burton, *The Joy of Writing,* p. 119, 121, 122, 125, 174, 303 and 257.

31 https://inaspaciousplace.wordpress.com/2012/07/05
the-comfortable-pew-a-few-problems/

By 1965, the Baby Boomers were rejecting the values of their parents; iconoclasm was the order of the day."

And a critical review it was, calling attention to "outmoded, inaccessible, irrelevant language and liturgy. The lessons," he says, "which, though beautifully phrased and intoned, might as well have been in a foreign tongue: the sermons had nothing to say."

Writing again in *The Comfortable Pew* Pierre Burton says, "Many people who no longer attend church, but who continue to call themselves Christian, give as a reason the fact that the service does nothing for them. The liturgy is 'dull and old-fashioned,' the phraseology unfamiliar, the words archaic, the sermons cliché-ridden and irrelevant to the times, the organ music 'square,' the congregation spiritless. One suspects that many of the in-group, who use old and worn-out phrases, are talking almost by rote, without having hacked through the thicket of cliché to get at the truth beneath. They really do not know what they are saying."

Though *The Comfortable Pew* was written in 1965, these problems certainly did not suddenly surface in the sixties. They had been in evidence much earlier than that. I am sure that the seeds of this criticism were already in evidence in the late '40's when Reba was wrestling with the question of her future in the church, but, as shown by her message titles, Pierre would have missed the mark in calling her sermons "cliché-ridden and irrelevant to the times." Had he heard her, he might have criticized her for her commitment to truth, but hardly for being boring. As a pastor, myself, I cannot help but believe that Reba found herself in a denomination with some of the problems described by Mr. Berton.

In this, she appears to follow a different path from her forerunner Lydia Gruchy. Lydia was able to persevere and find humour in her situation, with the result that she continued to receive high praise throughout her lifetime. Reba did not stay to receive those honours.

I am sure that Lydia Gruchy and many of her fellow ministers who sought to serve the Lord Jesus as faithfully as possible would strongly disagree with Mr. Berton, though her biographer, Patricia Wotton[32] has her own criticisms.

In her final chapter, "Reflections", which is worth the price of her book, Rev. Wotton states, "Today, the church continues to be an institution in a

---

32 Wotton, *With Love, Lydia,* p. 239 f.

time when institutions are decidedly out of vogue and past their prime, at least for the time being. Today, institutions tend to garner suspicion rather than unquestioning respect, and are often perceived as outdated, slow, and unresponsive, preoccupied with their own survival."

She continues, "From the hinterland of the prairies, the view is of a church obsessed with a corporate image of success, ensconced in the midst of the wealthy and powerful. What was once 'The United Church House' is now 'the United Church Head Office', and increasingly, a flow of legalistic policies, guidelines, and surveys from the National Church Office seem driven by fear and confusion, empty of the former depths and strength of faith. Some suggest, not entirely humorously, that where the United Church once had a God, it now has a lawyer.

"Despite the fact that the United Church has had many effective Moderators who, in their turn, have travelled miles and worked hard to reach out to Conferences and Presbyteries in the intent of giving a face to the wider church, it hasn't been enough. Many in local congregational ministry admit to feeling isolated and vulnerable, as the factors that have traditionally served to unite this church have been weakened or erased. The National United Church seems obsessed with the quest for an image of a church attractive to young people, belatedly, since it's been half a century since young people first began sliding away. The not-so-hidden motivation is a perceived last-ditch effort at institutional salvation."

While Lydia goes on to emphasize positive things which she sees happening, I think that Reba was reacting to some of these very factors, which were evident to her in 1950, as they were to myself in the mid-sixties. I would ascribe the problem to that which Reba saw developing from the time of her seminary training – the loss of faith in the true gospel of Christ.

Reba Leaves the Ministry:

What took place during these last years that led Reba to leave the ministry? I do not know. I can suspect that she may have experienced what we now call burnout. As mentioned above, I have always suspected that as a woman, she ran into "an old boys' club" and was perhaps made to feel that she was not really welcome and her preaching was too evangelical.

In the early seventies, I visited with a United Church minister in Sudbury, Ontario to whom I said, "I have heard that you are an evangelical United Church minister." He chuckled and said, "Well, in the eyes of my United Church brethren, I am an evangelical. In the eyes of your Baptist brother here in Sudbury, I am a liberal, so I get shot from both sides." Not an easy position to be in.

In answer to my speculation that Reba may have "burned out", Rev. Snyder [33] gives a thoughtful and welcome response.

> "As to confirmation about Reba suffering burnout, while I think it is entirely possible, I don't think the concept would have been part of the awareness in that era. I came dangerously close myself while serving in the same charge, but you would be hard pressed to find anyone there who was aware of my situation.
> "Besides, I would imagine that even if she was experiencing this, she would have felt tremendous pressure to hide any sign of weakness. She was a pioneer under constant scrutiny of those determined to prove she did not belong. The same pressure that may have led to burnout would drive her to conceal any evidence that it was happening to her.
>
> She must have been an incredibly strong-willed woman."
>
> Peace, Colin

Reba's final message as a United Church minister was preached April 23, 1950.

No sermon title is listed, but it was from Acts 7:54-8:50. It covers the martyrdom of Stephen with Saul holding the coats while Stephen cried out, "Look! I see the heavens opened and the Son of Man standing at the right hand of God." They stoned Stephen as he was calling on God, and saying, "Lord Jesus, receive my spirit. Lord do not charge them with this sin." The following chapter records the fact that Saul was consenting to his death and

---

33 Rev. Colin Snyder in email to Allen Hern, August 7, 2017. "You are free to quote me if you wish, but please be sure that it is perceived that it is supposition on my part. I have no real evidence to support it."

a great persecution arose against the church and they were all scattered, and went everywhere preaching the word. The next chapter records Saul's conversion to become the mighty Apostle Paul.

Did this message have any reference to Reba's resignation? There is no way of knowing.

Whatever the situation, Reba resigned on April 23, 1950, and did not seek further ministry.

What was her mindset? What were her thought patterns at this point? What led her to enter a convent? What was the full effect of her parents' shock and confusion at this point? These are questions to which I have no answers.

One of my regrets, as her biographer, is the failure of my wife and myself to explore these questions with Reba in the years in which we visited her in her retirement. What an opportunity we had to review with her those ministry years, and gain her reflections on preaching the gospel of Christ.

Reba was no shrinking violet. She remained to the end of her life a strong woman, with strong opinions on a wide variety of subjects. However, I believe my cousin was a conflicted woman, torn between her loyalty to the Lord Jesus and the liberalism which had for so many years been evident in her denomination.

We hope to learn more in "The In-Between Years."

CHAPTER EIGHT

The In Between Years

"Don't cry because it's over, smile because it happened."

— Dr. Seuss

So, having resigned from the ministry, what did she do and where did she go? I have no records to go on, but at 11 years of age, I had the impression of hushed tones as my parents discussed the fact that Reba had gone into a Roman Catholic Convent. I had the sense that Uncle Herb and Aunt Carrie were in shock, and probably in denial.

In that state, they enlisted the services of a man well known to Reba to visit her and to try to talk some sense into her. He failed, and in the convent she remained.

I have been unsuccessful in tracing the convent she entered. I had lovely correspondence with Kimberley Price, supervisor of disclosure at the Catholic Children's Aid of London and Middlesex in London, Ontario. In telling her of Reba's background, Kimberley said, "I feel close to her already. I will see what I can find."

In spite of that I was unable to learn more. A representative of the Sisters of St. Joseph in London, Ontario sent me a request for disclosure, but stated, "I have doubts that we can help in the case of someone who has left the congregation." I was therefore unable to discover how she spent the five years, from April, 1950 to late 1955. If my suspicion of burnout should be accurate, then those five years were perhaps involved in recovery from that condition. Judging from Mrs. Doyle's comments below, it appears that Reba actually became a Roman Catholic at that time. Did she simply attend the Catholic

Church? Or did she take classes to formalize her "conversion"? It sounds as though she may have done so.

During those years, Reba appears to have healed enough under the kindness and assistance of the sisters that she was able to step forward into a new future.

How fully did she enter into the daily lives of the sisters during those years? I cannot answer, but by late 1955 she applied successfully to the Catholic Children's Aid Society and began service under the leadership of Laura M. Doyle, the supervisor.

On June 8, 1956, her supervisor, Laura M. Doyle, filled out a Staff Evaluation, which helps us to catch a picture of her during this period. Her education is listed, including her three-year post-graduate course in theology.

Under 'Experience', her thirteen-year ministry is mentioned, but nothing is said about her time in the convent.

The second section of her evaluation is entitled: 'Performance of Worker'.

For six to seven months, she served as a caseworker in the Catholic Children's Aid Society in London, Ontario.[34] Miss Doyle states:

"Miss Hern is a genuine, warm, kindly, interested person. Because she likes people for their own worth, she accepts individual differences. She finds a different challenge in each age group of children.

"Her change of religion when she was a mature woman necessitated overcoming many prejudices. She moved from a recognized profession, bringing along a social viewpoint and a desire to help others to make effective use of their lives. Self-analysis had always been necessary in order to meet the requirements and expectations of her former profession. She realizes that all people have their own set of standards, which meet their needs more or less satisfactorily. She feels that in order to help people help themselves they must see themselves as they really are and that little can be accomplished with them until they reach this point."

Immediately, we see evidence of not just a change of occupation but a change of religion.

---

34 The following quotes are taken from the Staff Evaluation – Catholic Children's Aid Society June 6, 1956, Laura M. Doyle. I assume that this was an independent agency and not run by the nuns.

This would suggest that Reba had joined the Catholic Church. Throughout her journals, I find recurring references to Roman Catholicism, yet as we shall note, from the time she arrived in Nassau, she was not attending Roman Catholic services.

Even late in life, as my wife and I visited her in her retirement years, we saw evidences of a strong appreciation of the Catholic Church and of the Pope. She seemed to have felt that the Catholic Church had retained a sense of authority, which had been lost in non-Catholic religion. That being said, while she attended Catholic churches sporadically in the Vancouver area, as I will discuss later, she experienced another deep disillusionment during the Mount Cashel scandal that rocked that religion. Here is another evidence of the inner conflict with which she was so familiar.

Mrs. Doyle's staff evaluation continues:

"Miss Hern is very sensitive to the feelings of others, tactful on most occasions."

"Tactful on most occasions." That is an interesting observation in light of at least one comment made by Reba herself at a later date.

"Experience has taught her to make the best use of her time and to work planfully. This comes easily as she has spent a number of years in a public service. Through her experience in this agency, she knows its purposes, philosophy and legal framework. She has taken courses in social work, since her employment here, when time and personal plans permitted."

"Miss Hern uses good judgement, sees that, before case work can be started, she must find the beginning point and the cause.

"Miss Hern is jovial, friendly and sincere, which has made her relationship with workers good. Often, at much personal sacrifice, she has altered her plans and given a service to children who might otherwise suffer, physically or emotionally. She has given a good deal of her own time, cheerfully, without any intent of requiring compensation or recognition.

"It must have required a great deal of this worker to see a need for supervision, when she has always 'run her own show', even as a student missionary.

"Miss Hern was anxious to learn the mechanics of the job and asked many intelligent questions, discussed her difficulties and made every possible effort to use her knowledge to help children and foster parents see themselves constructively.

"Miss Hern is a mature person who has led a well-ordered life and, in many ways, is far ahead of the recent graduate from Social Work Schools. She thinks deeply and her plans are the result of a right mixture of theory and experience. Though the transfer from the ministry, and though a change of religion was charged with difficulties, she has come through and has a good foundation of the basic principles of social work.

"Miss Hern has lived life and in her various experiences she has known many kinds of people – hopeful, discouraged, prosperous, indigent, irresponsible, intellectual and illiterate. She has an analytical mind and endeavours to understand the behaviour of children and interpret their actions in terms of her own understanding.

"Miss Hern gets along well with people. They confide in her easily. She is well experienced in listening carefully and then picking up the interview point by point. Sometimes Miss Hern is inclined to be carried away with the feeling tone and is inclined to act impulsively.

"Miss Hern has an ability to transcribe warmth, interest, sympathy and good counsel in her letters to children and foster parents; business letters are clear and precise. She becomes very fond of the persons she likes and tends to over-identify. This, I feel is a carryover from her much longer experience in the ministerial role.

"Miss Hern has no difficulty in accepting hostility, anger, stolidity or impudence as a defense mechanism. She knows people and realizes when and where they need help. There are few people she can't reach.

"There is, generally, a very satisfactory relationship between Miss Hern, foster parents, and children. She is always concerned about anything that affects the child and is most interested and energetic about using every resource available to improve the child physically, morally and mentally.

"She plans thoughtfully and thoroughly for the child's education, changing environment when necessary, procuring reliable vocational guidance and inspiring the children by her own personal characteristics to become worthwhile people."

Although we have none of her own notes from this period, it is good to see this kind of assessment. It gives us better insight into her nature and character at this season of her life. Notice the appreciative comments about her personality. "Miss Hern is jovial, friendly and sincere, which has made her relationship with workers good." "Miss Hern is a mature person who has led a well-ordered life." "She has an analytical mind and endeavours to understand." "Miss Hern gets along well with people. They confide in her easily." "Miss Hern has an ability to transcribe warmth, interest, sympathy, and good counsel."

If my earlier assumption of burnout is in any way accurate, it certainly does not show up in the judgement of Mrs. Doyle as her supervisor. It is well, though, to remember that she had already spent almost five years in the convent during which she had opportunity to heal and prepare for a new profession while still carrying forward the benefits of her earlier ministry.

At the same time, Reba's strong personality shows through.

"Sometimes Miss Hern is inclined to get carried away with the feeling tone and is inclined to act impulsively. This I feel is a carryover from her much longer experience in the ministerial role." In other words, there were times in which Reba found it hard to operate within the confines of regulations. She was used to a leadership role and that may have gotten her into difficulty.

As the writer of her memoir, I am so thankful that we have this independent description of her person, her gifting, and her character. It helps to anchor us as we follow her to Nassau and as we read her more critical comments about the situation and the people involved in the school, the Ministry of Education and the Bahamas as a whole.

Having said that, it appears that she was now ready to consider another step in her life. The question now was, what would that next step be?

I have no idea how she heard of a teaching position in Nassau, in the Bahamas. She was not a trained teacher but the job was teaching Religious Knowledge in the Government High School. Surely with this background she was well qualified to take on that responsibility. Obviously, others thought so too, for her application was accepted and soon Reba was ready to head into an exciting new challenge which I have described in chapters one and two.

CHAPTER NINE

Visiting Reba's Stomping Grounds

"Never be afraid to sit awhile and think."

— Lorraine Hansberry

Having opened this book with two chapters about Reba arriving in Nassau, I led you through her childhood, youth, ministry life, and its sequel, all of which was a preparation for her new occupation.

Although Reba's coming to Nassau exposed her to many new experiences, the main reason she was there was to teach Religious Knowledge and English to the students of the Government High School. In Chapter One, I described her introduction to the black children in their blue and white uniforms, and the inadequate building in which the school was housed.

As I contemplated writing her story, I felt the need to talk to someone in Nassau who could give me firsthand information about her adopted homeland. After unsuccessful attempts, I talked to someone who knew just to whom I should speak. "You need to talk to Dr. Gail Saunders at the University of the Bahamas. She has the widest possible knowledge of Nassau and has written books about it."

I could just imagine the run-around I was about to receive, in calling a busy university, but I made the call. In explaining whom I was seeking, I heard, "Just a minute, and then a soft, gentle voice, 'Hello, this is Gail Saunders.'"

Amazing, and thus began a correspondence which led to a second professor at the University, Dr. Nicolette Bethel. Eventually, it led to the dream of visiting Nassau and my wife, Sheila, and I seeing that area for ourselves.

In February 2018, with a view to writing these memoirs, we visited Nassau and found ourselves, like Reba, in a new and different environment. We were anxious to actually see the city in which she had spent 16 years of her life.

Unlike Reba, flying in a fairly small Trans-Canada Airlines airplane from Toronto into the small and outdated Oakes Field in September, 1957, Sheila and I arrived on February 10, 2018 in a modern WestJet plane. We landed with anticipation at the very modern Nassau International Airport (Windsor Field).

Interestingly, this airfield was under construction when Reba landed in September of 1957. It was labour problems over taxi service to that airport which led directly to the 1958 General Strike as I reported in Chapter Two, 'Nassau in a time of change.'

Also, unlike Reba, we were arriving with a well-planned itinerary prepared by Expedia Cruise Ship Centers in Kamloops, BC. There are advantages to working with a travel agent. Of course, the disadvantage was the cost of the trip. A travel agent wants the client to have the best of everything and the cost of $450.00 per night would have shocked cousin Reba out of a year or two of growth, since she thought that a hotel of $15.00-$20.00 was 'expensive.' The benefit was that we knew where we were going and so caught a taxi to the all-inclusive Warwick Paradise Island Hotel. The second benefit was that everything was paid for in advance including all our sumptuous meals. We were not encouraged to tip the staff, since this was included.

Our first taste of island hospitality came from the black taxi driver who was very friendly and informative as he introduced us to the island. While we looked eagerly out the windows as he drove us the 18 miles to Paradise Island, he explained our surroundings with frequent repetitions of "You know what ah'm sayin?" It was an expensive ride: $42.00, but worth it to listen to our first Bahamian.

We arrived at the luxurious Warwick hotel, and began to get settled. Four or five restaurants were available, of which we used just the main dining room.

The staff were wonderful. I was surprised at how well-spoken the entire staff was. Unlike our taxi driver, who delighted us with his "island" accent, there was very little evidence in the dining room of a Bahamian or Nassau dialect in these young adults serving us. They were not 'in your face', but they were always near at hand, fully aware of every need we might have.

We served ourselves from the almost endless selection of foods from salads through multiple possibilities of main courses to numerous choices of desserts. We were free to go back for more if we wished. As soon as we finished with our plates, the girls, or fellows, were there to remove them while we got new plates for dessert. Coffee, tea, juice, pop, and if we had wanted, wine was all available, without limit.

As Sheila says, "On Sunday, it was odd not to go to church," but we had not had opportunity to find out what was available. Paradise Island is separated from Nassau proper by a fairly wide waterway, but tied to the main island by two side-by-side bridges. The churches were in the city, not on the island where we were.

We met a couple from Iowa who are believers in the Lord Jesus. That was a treat in itself. They told us of a 'water-taxi' which goes from a wharf near the bridges to the straw market in Nassau. They said it is not easy to get into the boat, but men help you in and out. At $8.00 return per person, it is much cheaper than a taxi. After talking to them we returned to our rooms to watch the Olympics.

On Monday, I was able to contact Dr. Nicolette Bethel, but not Dr. Gail Saunders. Arrangements were made to meet for lunch on Tuesday.

After those arrangements were made, we booked a city tour. This tour took us to Fort Charlotte.[35]

Located one mile west of downtown Nassau, just off West Bay Street, it sits on a hill overlooking the far west end of the harbour, commanding an impressive view of Paradise Island, Nassau, and the harbour.

Built in 1788 by Lord Dunmore, the fort was named after the wife of King George III, Queen Saharia Charlotte. The middle bastion, Fort Stanley, and the western portion, Fort D'Arcy were added later. The fort has a moat, dungeons, underground passageways, and 42 cannons, which have never been fired in an act of aggression.

We found it interesting but not really impressive.

As we continued to tour through the city, we heard the story of hospitals, governors' homes, and government buildings all painted in pastel shades according to the function of the building.

---

35 https://www.bahamas.com/vendor/fort-charlotte

We passed the Methodist Church, which Reba had attended. We also saw many old houses, some quite decrepit. It was obviously an old city.

By contrast, the University, which we drove past, was new and modern, having just been upgraded from a college to the status of a university in 2016.

But having seen a bit of the area, we need to get back to our reason for being there. We were there to get a better understanding of Reba and her relationship with her surroundings.

You remember the description of the Government High School as Reba first experienced it which I reported in Chapter One. She was in that building for three years.

But that changed. Marjorie Davis, who taught with Reba at GHS from the time she arrived from Canada, remembers her well. Although she is now 91 years of age, Marjorie recalls clearly the move to the new school.

"In 1960, she would have been among the 20 teachers and 300 plus students involved in the relocation of the school to a new campus less than two miles inland to Poinciana Drive."

From another source, I find that Reba helped to fundraise for the new school. This is the school, which has now been incorporated into the University and was no doubt a great improvement upon the old Methodist Chapel.

The question we wanted answered was, 'What kind of a teacher was my cousin?' Was she well prepared to teach Religious Knowledge? Did she have the temperament and personality to have a beneficial influence on these high school students? Was she able to adapt to this new culture into which she was now thrust? To answer these questions, I wanted to hear from one or more of her former students.

Miss Davis forwarded to me a letter from one such student.

Reba Hern, As I remember her:

"She was gentle, patient and kind.

"With her hair impeccably coiffed, sensible low-heeled shoes and her genteel ladylike walk, she was different.

"Firstly, she was not the usual teachers from Great Britain, who were looking for the easy life in the sun with little regard for our futures, Ms. Hern was different. It always fascinated me the way her face would transform when speaking about religion or more importantly to me, the classic works of literature. For those of us who loved to read, it was like taking a journey without ever leaving the island!

"One day, I was sitting by the "huts", reading a book. (*The Godfather* by Mario Puzo)

"She sat down next to me and asked me if my mother knew that I was reading that particular book (I was thirteen years old). I told her that I asked my mother to buy it for me. She looked surprised that my mother would buy such a racy book for a teenager. I explained to her that I was not interested in Mills and Boon's romance novels because their plot was always the same. I had her then! She then asked me if I would write a book report about the novel explaining the plot and what I had learned from it. Two weeks later, I gave her the report. The next day she came looking for me and asked me if I would come and talk to her about the report.

"When I got there, she said to me that I should explore a career in teaching English. I laughed and told her that teachers were too poor and did not make enough money. Sadly, she agreed with me but extracted my promise to consider it.

"That year, I had signed up for BJC English Literature and one of the books was *Julius Caesar*. There were not enough students who had signed up for the exam and so it was dropped from the school schedule.

"Immediately, Ms. Hern volunteered to tutor me for the exam. I read through her copy of the book and she reviewed it chapter by chapter with me, highlighting the salient points of each chapter for the exam. I never studied outside of those sessions with Ms. Hern for that exam. Needless to say, she was bursting with pride when I got a distinction in the exam!

"Over the next school year, we studied everything every Wednesday afternoon. From the Bible to even Mills and Boon novels (I still hate them!). Sadly, Ms. Hern left after that year.

"I am very grateful to all of my teachers at The Government High school, for teaching us the things that were never in books, like character, integrity, honesty and principles. I am especially grateful to Ms. Hern for expanding my love of reading and learning!

"P.S. She also taught me that a lady always wears low comfortable shoes and that a string of pearls were the only accessory that a lady needed!"

How thankful I am for this description of my cousin not only as a teacher but as a compassionate, caring individual who took a personal interest in her students.

Yet another former student, Dierdre Donathan remembers her in this way:

"I was in Ms. Hern's English class. Unfortunately, the only thing I recall about those classes was that a few of the students would totally ignore her as she was teaching and some were a bit disruptive at times; and Ms. Hern did not have a good command on executing

control. She was tough. She would turn red when she was angry. Her revenge would come when you did not pass her tests.

"Her hair was always immaculately coiffed.

"She was a wonderful teacher. It is because of her dedication that we did well in English and developed a love of reading: She was a gentle quiet woman with a love for two of the most boring subjects outside of Latin."

A fellow teacher, Jean Knowles, writes about her:

"She was a very quiet and efficient teacher with no disciplinary problems. I know she was kind and did the Christian thing in identifying a very needy boy. He had sores from malnutrition so Reba brought sandwiches for him every day (there were no school meals then,

so without her interest he would have found the schoolwork very difficult). She may have done this for other kids too but this case I saw with my own eyes.

"She attended all the school functions and parties given by some of the teachers.

"One thing I noted, she did not seem to understand the Bahamian society. We were all a congenial bunch - laughing and joking with one another regardless of race. This did not extend to romancing - whites and blacks did not usually marry. Reba seemed to think the friendliness might lead to something more as it did with English teachers but not Bahamian teachers."

Jean also writes: "I do remember that Reba taught RE to an A level class and she was very disappointed with her most prominent student who went off on a tangent answering the questions from a fundamentalist church's teaching and disregarding what she had taught him. See, you have prompted me to remember that. A-Level students are the group over 18. They have fulfilled the GE schooling requirements and today might do the work in a junior college, which we didn't have at that time."

As her cousin and biographer, I replied by e-mail, "Reba began life with a very Evangelical position, I believe, but I think her experience brought about a change, so I expect that she may have taught a more liberal brand perhaps also touched by Catholicism." Whether that was the case or not, I am not really in a position to say definitely.

Another of her former students, Anita Dillet also shares her memories.

Subject: Memories of Miss Reba Hern

"Hello Mr. Hern,

"I am happy to share memories of your relative, Miss. Reba Hern.

"Mrs. Hern taught Religious Knowledge at Government High School in 1960 when I was a first form student there. She was a sociable person who was always approachable. Her classes were not too structured as there were times to discuss matters arising from the Scripture at hand. We found out that she was a Reverend, but I cannot remember what her religious affiliation was. She preached at certain weekend services at the church she attended.

"There was a student in our class who hailed from Harbor Island, one of the islands in the Bahamian archipelago. Natives of that area add 'H' sound to words that begin with vowels and they would drop the 'H' sound to words that began with the letter 'H'. So, it was hilarious at times when she called him to stand and read a portion of the lesson in the Bible. He didn't mind the laughter and Mrs. Hern had to stop the class many times to bring order to the situation. 'Girls, please stop the laughter.'"

"But Miss Hern, he doesn't mind', we would say – 'in fact he was having a great time laughing at himself.'

"On occasion she would come to class a few minutes late and we would be having a great time until the sound of her shoes could be heard coming down the tiled corridor because we knew the sound of her steps in her high heeled shoes. Someone near the door would shout out, "Sexy Reba coming, be quiet'. Her gait was somewhat stiff and her bosom stood out as she walked, hence the nickname, Sexy Reba."

"Her methodology was excellent. Her passes in the General Certificate of Education, 'O' level were a testimony to her instructions and the good rapport she had with her students.

"There were always many of us around her desk asking questions of life and personal matters.

"As I entered the third and fourth forms, I had to make a choice between Religious Knowledge and English Literature. I chose Literature and my days with "Sexy Reba" came to a conclusion but warm memories of her still come to mind when I recall Miss Hern's classes at the Government High School.

Best Regards

Anita Bosfield Dillet"

Ah! Sexy Reba!! Now there's something I hadn't heard before!! As for her bosom standing out, that description is quite apt as she was a full-figured woman. From these personal testimonies, I received the answer to my questions. Yes, my cousin was well prepared to teach both Religious Knowledge and English to the students of Government High School. Without doubt her university education and her years in ministry had given her all the tools needed to be a competent instructor. Her time as a social worker with the Catholic Children's Aid Society had given her the compassion and the skills to deal with youth who may not always have been willing to receive her help.

On Tuesday, February 13, we found our way to Le Petite Gourmet restaurant, which is just as its name suggests – a little gourmet restaurant. At a small table, surrounded by others, we met Dr. Gail Saunders, with whom I had been corresponding. Dr. Saunders founded the Bahamian National Archives of which she was the director for 33 years from 1971-2004. As a historian, Dr. Saunders had written the two-volume *Islanders in the Stream* from which I have quoted, plus numerous other books. She presented us with an autographed copy of her latest description of the Bahamas: *Race and Class in the Colonial Bahamas, 1880 – 1960*.

Over lunch at Le Petite Gourmet, we also met Dr. Nicolette Bethel, a Bahamian teacher, writer, anthropologist and full-time lecturer in Social Science at the University of the Bahamas, with whom I had also corresponded. Both of these ladies are professors at the University of the Bahamas. Together, these delightful Bahamian ladies answered our questions about the

Nassau in which Reba had lived. Both confirmed Reba's suggestions about politics, education and the division between blacks and whites in Nassau at that time.

Dr. Saunders would have been a 13-year-old student in 1957 when Reba came to GHS, although she was not in Reba's classes. In 1962, at 18 years old, she was one of four women chosen to represent the Bahamas in international sports competition at the Central American and Caribbean games, as a member of the sprint relay team.

Does she remember Reba? Did Reba know this highly intelligent and gifted young woman? Not on a personal level.

From 1966, Gail was in England taking her B.A and post-graduate studies. She then studied under Michael Craton at the University of Waterloo to receive her doctorate. (I mentioned Dr. Craton earlier as having taught with Reba for about four years.) She was therefore out of the country for much of Reba's time, but the books Dr. Saunders co-authored with Michael Craton confirm everything that Reba had written in her journals.

On Friday, I was determined to visit the university, and to see the school where Reba taught.

We again took the water taxi to the city. This was an interesting experience, because each ferry holds up to about 50 people. On each ferry, a 'guide' keeps up a well-rehearsed patter, about the history of the buildings and the various celebrities who have lived here. Before landing, each guide emphasizes that he is not employed by the ferry and that he will welcome any tips that he receives as this is the way he makes his living. He probably does fairly well.

We had been told what bus to take, but we couldn't see street signs until we found that the street names were on the curbs. Fortunately, a couple of Nausauvian ladies were waiting for the same bus and told us where to leave the bus.

As we walked the halls of the University, we met Prestonia Wallace, another professor at the University of the Bahamas, who graciously showed us around. Dr. Saunders was not in her office, nor were there many students in the hallways. Prestonia also showed us the Government High School, which now seems to be built into the University as a whole. The whole University and school is finished in cream coloured stucco and looks very attractive.

But Prestonia did not stop there. She insisted on driving us back to the straw market where we could again board the water-taxi. Along the way she picked up Paul Fernander, a former student at GHS, who said, "I don't remember being in her class but she was a gentle soul and I think what Debbie said is true: she was a neat motherly woman and was attentive to those who tried and wanted to learn." Paul demonstrated that he had known my cousin for he was able to describe her perfectly.

As we arrived back at the waterfront, five cruise ships were in port so many people were on the streets. What a delightful day!

After we returned home, these delightful people put us in touch by email with several others including Patricia Rodgers, the daughter of Anatol Rodgers, who with her husband Kenneth were friends of Reba. Anatol went on to become the headmistress of GHS, only the second black woman to achieve that status.

In her journals, Reba speaks of her involvement in many other areas than teaching. One of those areas was the Red Cross. Again, Miss Davis writes, "During her tenure at the School, Miss Hern had the responsibility for the School's Junior Red Cross Link and directed the Link in making a 'Scrapbook' which was ultimately presented to the Red Cross Headquarters in England."

In all of this, we get a picture of a woman whose varied experience equipped her well for the task of teaching in her adopted country. Our week in Nassau came to a close, but we were so happy to have been able to visit Reba's adopted country. Along the way, my wife fell in love with Nassau, with the result that we would welcome the opportunity to visit the island of New Providence, the city of Nassau, and Paradise Island again. "You know what ah'm sayin?"

CHAPTER TEN

Conflict and Loss

"Peace is not the absence of conflict; it is the ability to handle conflict by peaceful means."

— Ronald Reagan.

Although we have no journal records from 1958-59 to 1966, we can fill in many of those changes from other materials.

As I have stated in Chapter Two, there was no doubt that the Bahamas were changing.

For one thing the population was rapidly increasing. Saunders and Craton show that in 1953, the population[36] for the whole of the Bahamas was 83,841, made up of almost 11,000 Whites (13%), almost 62,000 Blacks (73%) and 12,000 Mixed (14%).

By 1963, it was over 130,000, and by 1970, the population had almost doubled in 17 years to 170,000. Most of this increase was during Reba's years there. Changes were happening in other ways. That small white population had been the ruling class prior to 1953. As a black Methodist minister said, "I doubt if there is anywhere else on earth masquerading as a 'democracy' with a less representative government. Instead of 'government of the people for the people,' we have 'exploitation of the many for the privileged by the few.'"

By 1953 the blacks were stirring. Efforts to organize a formal political party to oppose Bay Street and its practices led to the formation of the Progressive Liberal Party (PLP) in September, 1953.

---

36   Craton and Saunders, *Islanders in the Stream,* p. 196, 197.

"The Progressive Liberal Party hopes to show that your big man and your little man, your black, brown and white man of all classes, creed, and religions in this country can combine and work together in supplying sound and successful political leadership which has been sadly lacking in the Bahamas."

The two key figures were Milo Butler, with his emotive Baptist-preacher style, and the more cerebral Lynden Pindling.[37]

With the rise of the P.L.P., the Bay Street clique also organized into the United Bahamian Party (UBP) in 1958. That was brought about by the 1958 General Strike as I reported in Chapter Two.

"During 1960, the PLP made important recruits among the small group of middle-class black professionals and almost doubled its representation in the House of Assembly, which increased political, racial, and class tensions. Mixed race and black persons benefited greatly from the improved standards of the Government High School which moved out of its cramped quarters into a modern purpose-built building at Oakes Field, becoming a crucial factor in the growth of the professional non-white middle class. Other high schools, operated by the Anglican and Roman Catholic churches were also helping to raise the standards of the non-white population. Women obtained the vote in 1961 though the campaign exhibited an unprecedented racial polarization and bitterness." [38]

Reba was there through all of these changes, but, lacking journals, we can't know what she was experiencing. This is a major loss for our knowledge of her life.

There was an election that temporarily set back the progress of the PLP, which lost two seats, likely due to "a fear of the consequences of black majority rule, shared not only by the white minority, and the non-white middle classes but by many of the blacks themselves."[39] It is noteworthy that women voted for the first time in the 1962 election.

Meanwhile, Reba's family life was also changing.

Since writing this, I have discovered four letters from Reba's sister Carrie, written in the week of November 9 – 14, 1960 about their mother's illness.

---

37   Craton and Saunders, *Islanders in the Stream,* p. 308

38   Craton and Saunders, *Islanders in the Stream,* p. 312.

39   Craton and Saunders, *Islanders in the Stream,* p. 314.

November 9,1960: "Dear Reba, Here I am in the Sault again. Mother is back in hospital. She is having a 2 ½ hour operation today... She has been having pain in her leg...and the Xray showed that the bone is dead and didn't heal around the pin at all... When Dad came, she was really down."

November 11, 1960: "Dear Reba, I know you will be anxious to hear about mother. Yesterday morning we went in for a while. She opened her eyes and recognized me. Her old eyes lighted up. She was so glad to see me. It is hard for her to talk. She is a very sick woman. I'm fine, myself although I had to miss my check-up at the clinic." (We found out later that she herself was dealing with cancer at this time.)

"Really, Reba, you and I are very changeable and I think maybe I was happier with Wilbur as a minister's wife then I would have been, living my life in Sault Ste. Marie and trying to fit into this fundamentalist group here. It is rough on Wilbur but he needs a bit of rough usage once in a while."

November 14, 1960: "This is the story as I see it. Mother is over surgery and will likely be home in a few weeks. She won't ever walk again and hates the wheelchair... I tried to get Dad to face up to the fact and look what I have on my hands!!

"Let's forget all of my upsets of the past three months. Wilbur has lots of faults but so do we all."

November 17, 1960: "Mother is coming along very well now and the Doctor assures me that she will be fine... So far as you are concerned, I think mother and dad are going to be fine and they don't want you to come home for Christmas unless you want to. On the other hand, you never know when you may be called home, so you might be advised to wait till then."

During 1962, my Aunt Carrie, Reba's mother died in Sault Ste. Marie, Ontario. I have no doubt that Reba came home for the funeral but I wasn't there to see it. I was away in Teacher's College in North Bay, Ontario that year, and my brother does not have a memory of that event or of Reba's presence so we continue to base our understanding on outside sources. No doubt there was a sense of loss in that death.

The 1962 election victory gave the United Bahamian Party the opportunity to take advantage of the willingness of the British government to grant internal self-government[40] under the responsible government system.

In 1963, Constitutional talks in London led to self-government and a new constitution coming into effect on January 7, 1964, a proud moment for all Bahamians.

Though stunned by its 1962 defeat, the PLP soon recovered and moved forward with its own organization. "Politically astute and charismatic, Lynden Pindling also [41] showed personal moderation and pragmatism, which combined with his knowledge of constitutional matters to make him a successful leader."

A snap election called by the ruling UBP party, on January 10, 1967, in hopes that it would "catch the opposition unprepared," backfired.

In the years immediately following, the PLP gained in power and the black PLP party achieved a coalition government.

"For more than a year, the PLP government[42] was on trial. But it came through triumphantly, thanks to the moderation and shrewdness of its leaders, the almost uninterrupted improvement in the economy," and disgust at an investigation into casino licensing by the United Bahamian Party.

Thus, 1963 to 1973 was a decade of radical changes. As Craton and Saunders say, "No other ten-year period in Bahamian history saw so much economic, political, and social change as that which began with Bay Street's last general election victory and ended with the achievement of Bahamian independence under the all black PLP government."

Recognizing the inadequacy of the Bahamian educational system, the government set out to Bahamianize education, upgrading school buildings, adding new secular and coeducational secondary schools, and increasing the Bahamian content of the curricula. But as Craton and Saunders point out, education continued to be more dependent on expatriate teachers mainly from Britain, plus a minority of Canadians and black West Indians. However,

---

40 Craton and Saunders, *Islanders in the Stream,* p. 337.

41 Gail Saunders, *Race and Class in the Colonial Bahamas:* 1880 – 1960, 2016, p. 250.

42 Ibid. p. 346.

as Reba makes clear, the Bahamian emphasis made life more difficult for all expatriate teachers, of which she was one.

In spite of these difficulties, it was a time of rapid growth and development, "the creation of a free port, industrial complex, luxury hotel, and residential area extending over the central part of Grand Bahama."[43]

A relatively new development called Freeport–Lucaya,[44] saw spectacular progress in the middle sixties. A fine modern clinic, library, private schools and churches, the best roads in the Bahamas, the largest and most modern electricity, water and sewage facilities, a deep-water harbour, and an airport capable of taking the largest jets were all part of this progress. Claims were made that Freeport–Lucaya, "with two thousand hotel beds, hundreds of marina berths, docking for cruise liners, and five eighteen-hole golf courses (more than in all the rest of the Bahamas) was already capable of handling a million tourists a year."

Now, at last, in 1966, we have one of her journals, which helps us to a better understanding of what is happening in her personal life.

January 1. 1966: "This year began at the British Colonial Hotel. I was part of a delightful dinner party given by Mr. and Mrs. Greenwold of Syracuse, New York, friends of Anatol Rodgers.

"They, along with their daughter Janice, spent last Sunday on Ken Rodger's boat. I was there also on the fishing expedition. Then the Rodgers had the same group for supper on Thursday evening. I was included. We had a lovely New Year's dinner. A pink lady first, lobster cocktail, filet mignon, and a cup of Marrons. This was accompanied by champagne. Around midnight there was a small floorshow. I slept at Mrs. Munroe's, then got home about 7 a.m. It was a most pleasant beginning for the New Year."

It is interesting to read this reference to the Rodgers. Anatol Rodgers was a black fellow teacher with whom Reba, at that time, was obviously good friends.

"The next day, around 11, friends Oliver and Margaret Hunter came to my house, bringing the Greenwolds. After 12, Martin Pounder arrived and 7 of us sat down to dinner. I had a large bottle of white Dubonnet for the wine.

---

43   Saunders, *Race and Class in the Colonial Bahamas*, p. 324.

44   Ibid p. 327.

After dinner, we had coffee in the demi-tasse and later eggnog and rum and still later tea and Christmas cake. I enjoyed very much having all these folks."

Reba did not identify Martin Pounder but in her book, *Race and Class in the Bahamas*, Gail Saunders tells us that Martin Pounder was the Caribbean representative for London's Trade Union Congress.[45] He first came to the Bahamas to give advice to the Taxi Cab Union and PLP. leaders prior to the 1958 General Strike. Along with Pindling and others, Pounder was one of those who also helped to negotiate a settlement. I am glad to learn more about this man who became a good friend.

"Martin Pounder invited me for supper at the Chinese Rici House where we had one order between us of lobster chow Mein. It was just exactly right after all the heavy meals. I got back home around 1 a.m. Altogether, it has been the best New Year's I have ever had.

January 8: "Today Miss Ella Jorden, Director of the Red Cross, moved in with me. A few days later, Martin Pounder invited me on a moonlight cruise on the Tropic Bird. We left the Yacht Haven at 7:30 - a nice night. We went around Paradise Island. The boat stopped off at Cabbage Beach and everyone had hamburgers, extra good in the sea air."

As the rise of the Progressive Liberal Party had begun with great changes in government since 1958, so there was a changing of the guard at the Government High School. The days of headmasters and teachers coming from England was drawing to a close with coloured people taking their place. Cecil Bethel was appointed as headmaster, a position for which Reba felt he did not have the ability. In turn, he appointed his favourites, some of whom, she felt were not suited for the leadership they were given. At the same time, the Ministry of Education was abandoning the high standard which had characterized the Government High School, flooding it with pupils who were not in her mind suitable to this type of education.

During these nine years at the Government High School, Reba had watched many of the changes taking place. Craton and Saunders acknowledge these pressures. "Most of the problems of Bahamian education under the PLP. stemmed from the very rapidity of its expansion and from underfunding....

---

45 http://sirrandolfawkes.com/yahoo_site_admin/assets/docs/The_Faith_That_
    Moved_the_Moutain.252193642.pdf

Undoubtedly mistakes were made through overenthusiasm, inexperience, and mismanagement."

In 1966, Reba wrote, "These have been very interesting days at school. The feeling against the expatriates is mounting fast in this colony. It is starting to catch the teachers at GHS. I may be caught in this myself."

She felt that a real change was taking place, which was to the detriment of the educational process. The wheels were beginning to come off the bus.

Teachers began leaving the school. Lou Morgan (from England) was let know that there was no future for him in the Bahamas.

"How stupid these English are who thought they would be thoroughly accepted by the Negroes and trusted them. At heart Cec. Bethel is out for the Bahamians and not for the English.

"Everywhere the English are going under. A White Paper on defense shows that England can no longer defend her Empire and must be helped by the US. She is pulling out of all her bases in the East."

Reba found herself caught between two groups. On the one hand, she felt that things were deteriorating under Bahamian rule. Yet, her housemates, like Ella Jordan, were women who were very English and very set in their ways, who thought England and the English ways were the only right way, and Reba felt herself put down by them. As a Canadian, she was neither fish nor fowl.

On a personal level as she entered 1966, she received word that her father was in ill health. But on January 21, she received a letter from her dad.

This, of course was my Uncle Herb Hern. I remember him from my boyhood, as a tense and somewhat irritable man. At that time, he was a millwright at the Pulp Mill in Sault Ste. Marie. But after his retirement, he appeared to soften a great deal. His wife, my Aunt Carrie, loved the water. He bought a fully equipped cottage at Pine Island, on Lake Huron, not because he liked boating and fishing, but because Carrie did. She was a few years older than him and in her later years, he gave himself utterly to her care. He was utterly heartbroken when she died in 1962.

"Dad writes to say he will arrive in Nassau January 29 as he was feeling much better."

During that week, Reba's father arrived from Sault Ste. Marie, Ontario.

"Dad arrived at 12:35 and seems remarkably well. In the evening, Ella had a dinner party: including Mr. and Mrs. Mooney Sr., Nigel Mooney their son who has a responsible position in Barclay's Bank, Mr. and Mrs. Hubert Knowles, the chief administrator at the hospital. There were also Mr. and Mrs. Bosh, the permanent secretary for finance, Martin Pounder, and the 3 of us."

What this points up is that during these nine years, Reba had begun to cultivate relationships with some of the more prominent people on the island. During the next two months, she and her father responded to a variety of invitations and she hosted dinner parties for various people, but all was not well.

"I came home very low. Dad's presence here doesn't help. I can never open up and really talk to Dad about anything. He and Mother had me so crushed and broken by their constant criticism and he is still the same. They cared nothing about my feelings or happiness. The whole idea was to keep me the little girl dominated by them. I have the upper hand on Dad now, and I must see that I keep it.

"If I try to discuss anything with him, he will always go quiet if I get enthusiastic. He lived much too long with my mother to make a companion in any way to me."

What was it that brought about the animosity shown in the above remark?

I am not sure why Reba felt so put down by her parents during these years. Perhaps it could be related to her leaving the ministry and entering a convent but its roots probably lie much deeper than this. Long after she had retired to Tsawwassen, British Columbia, Reba claimed that it was her mother's idea that she would become a minister in the United Church. If this were even remotely true, it might have played a part in her traumatic exit from the ministry, perhaps involving a nervous breakdown, combined with her parents' disapproval of her entry into a convent. Whatever the case, something had obviously placed a severe strain on their relationship. We'll explore more of this in a later chapter.

Tension was also obvious in the strained relationship which existed between her and her twin sister Carrie. Even though she proved herself throughout her life to be a strong and capable woman, I suspect that Reba carried with her a deep sense of inferiority. This showed up in her feeling that each of her housemates were always trying to dominate her.

In many ways, I feel that she was a conflicted woman – a strong personality, but subject to feelings of inferiority. In that, she was not unlike many of us who read this book.

"On April 2, Dad is to leave. It will be a relief to see him go. On Sunday morning he had a funny spell in the night. He awakened very cold and began to shake. This lasted for an hour, but he recovered enough to take the plane."

At last, he was gone, and in spite of these negative feelings, she felt the visit had gone well.

Apart from that personal concern, Reba was watching the events around her. Always a keen observer, she turned her attention once again to the local situation.

"These are interesting days in Nassau. There is the threat of the coloured people with their rapidly growing nationalism. The Negroes in the House of Assembly are blasting the policy of bringing Englishmen here as permanent secretaries. From every part of the world the English are being driven back into their own homeland. It looks as though it will happen here as well.

"But the English don't want to go home. They have so much better salaries here and living conditions are away above what they would have in England."

It was not only her family situation and the changes in Nassau, which held her attention. World conditions did not escape her attention.

Just at this time, there broke upon the world the "God Is Dead" theory.

On April 8, 1966, *Time Magazine* produced a magazine cover with the words in bold red letters "Is God Dead?" set against a black background.

The associated story was entitled: 'Theology: Toward a Hidden God'. I quote:

"Is God dead? The three words represent a summons to reflect on the meaning of existence. No longer is the question the taunting jest of skeptics for whom unbelief is the test of wisdom and for whom Nietzsche is the prophet who gave his answer a century ago. Even within Christianity, now confidently renewing itself in spirit as well as form, a small band of radical theologians has seriously argued that the churches must accept the fact of God's death, and get along without him. How does the issue differ from the age-old assertion that God does not and never did exist?

"The current death-of-God group believes that God is indeed absolutely dead but proposes to carry on and write a theology without *theos*, without God.

"If nothing else, the Christian atheists are waking the churches to the brutal reality that the basic premise of faith—the existence of a personal God, who created the world and sustains it with his love—is now subject to profound attack."[46]

"Death of God theology refers to a range of ideas by various theologians and philosophers that try to account for the rise of secularity and abandonment of traditional beliefs in God. They posit that God has either ceased to exist or in some way accounted for such a belief. Although theologians since Friedrich Nietzsche have occasionally used the phrase "God is dead" to reflect increasing unbelief in God, the concept rose to prominence in the late 1950s and 1960s, before waning again. The Death of God movement is sometimes technically referred to as theothanatology, deriving from the Greek *theos* (God) and *thanatos* (death). The main proponents of this radical theology included the Christian theologians Gabriel Vahanian, Paul Van Buren, William Hamilton, John Robinson, Thomas J. J. Altizer, Mark C. Taylor, John D. Caputo, the rabbi Richard L. Rubenstein, and Peter Rollins."

Reba was a thinker, and in response to the God is Dead philosophy she wrote, "As I thought about that, it seemed to me it is not God who is dead but the Church. I often wonder if I am doing the right thing by going to church at all."

Here, once again, we see the evidences of a conflicted person. I have the sense that her background of experience had left her seriously jaded, and her present church situation was not meeting the deep need of her heart. And yet, here is the evidence that Reba still retains faith.

She speaks often of "the teachings of Jesus of Nazareth" and in her emotional struggle, she seems to feel that no church or denomination was rightly representing Him. "The result has been that the Christian Church has not ministered to a sweet, simple faith that is humble and unassuming, but rather to a cursed pride where there is really no faith and God is dead."

46 "Is God Dead?" Time Magazine, April 8, 1966, Vol. 87, No. 14

In July, 1966 she received a letter from Aunt Alice, her dad's sister. Her dad had had a fall and was in hospital. "X-rays show a large mass in the bowel and the doctor is sure it is cancer. He is to be operated on this week." She booked a flight on the next plane to Ontario.

"I got the plane to the Soo and Wilbur met me at the airport. In the afternoon and evening, I went to the hospital. Dad is a very sick man."

In the night she was called to the hospital. He was very near death, but soon the crisis passed.

For days, Herb's condition went up and down, sometimes alert and bright, sometimes very low. The doctors told them that there was nothing they could do and that it was terminal.

Meanwhile tensions seemed to have been taking place in the house where Wilbur and Carrie and their daughter Brenda were living as well as Reba.

As we have seen before, Reba seems to have been convinced that the others were seeking to have an advantage over her. Whether or not this was true, it appears that the twin sisters were at odds with one another, and it was obviously an uncomfortable time. It is sad when this happens in any family, especially when there is such a need to be reconciled to one another in the face of the imminent death of a loved one. Where was the evidence of the peace promised by our Saviour in John 14:27? "Peace I leave with you, my peace I give to you; not as the world gives do I give to you. Let not your heart be troubled, neither let it be afraid." And again, in Philippians 4:7, "the peace of God, which surpasses all understanding, will guard your hearts and minds through Christ Jesus."

On August 6th, 1966, Uncle Herb passed away.

"At the funeral, Carrie, for the first time broke down and cried. Wilbur was in his glory. He was talking to this one and that one and making himself so congenial. The rest of the family were very much in the background."

Reba stayed on in the Sault, carrying out the terms of her dad's will, the disposition of the assets, the sale of 157 Cathcart and two other homes owned by her father.

At the end of August, she flew back to Nassau.

"My Canadian summer is over. On Wednesday evening I was at the Rodgers (Anatol and Kenneth). I talked to Kenneth about Dad. He told me dad had died of malignant peritonitis, and how the tissue had been broken down by the disease. I brought up the fact that Dad must have known he had this trouble when he was in Nassau. Kenneth said, "He wanted to enjoy himself as long as he could, and he was right."

"This settled all my worries about Dad's death. His doctors did what was right and he lived his life as he wanted to the end."

And so, she entered again into the routine of school and of social engagements. She saw Ella, her housemate off to Canada and to England, and joined up with a new lady, Nan Dumbell, moving to a new apartment.

"We are getting settled in the apartment, a nice apartment but not a home to me. It just isn't what I want. And oh, I hate this heat! At times I feel I can't endure it. I long for the crisp cold of Canada. How I would welcome the snow and ice. I loathe this everlasting summer."

As I read these words, I feel for Reba. At this stage of her life, she was not a happy woman. She seems to be completely disillusioned. Although she continued to attend the Methodist Church, I am not sure that she was receiving the benefit of faith. How much she needed to really experience again the reality which I believe she had once known as expressed in Colossians 3:15: "And let the peace of God rule in your hearts, to which also you were called in one body; and be thankful."

Conflict and loss: a reality in Nassau; a reality in England; and a reality in the life of my cousin, Reba Hern.

CHAPTER ELEVEN

More Challenges

**"Our ability to handle life's challenges is a measure of
the strength of character."**

— Les Brown

As we have already seen, my cousin faced many challenges in life. She had faced those challenges in ministry, and she faced those challenges while living in Nassau.

But although Reba's journals show a woman who was deeply conflicted about her position at the Government High School, and living in Nassau in general, her notebooks also reveal a woman with a very active social life. The Government High School was not the totality of her life.

Many social events are recorded with Reba both entertaining and being entertained.

January 1, 1968: "I began the New Year at Blackbeard's Tavern on Bay St. in Nassau. We were all drinking champagne and rattling our noisemakers. About 1:30 we went on to another party at Julia and Terry Smith's where we stayed for about an hour. There were many coloured people at this party. This made me realize that in spite of the Negro government, there are few coloured people at most of the places to which I go socially. At Blackbeards, there were only two tables with Negroes. It was 3 a.m. when I got home."

As I continue to read my cousin's journals, I can't help but notice the changes which have taken place in her life. She certainly was active on the social scene. Parties at Anatol and Kenneth Rodgers', visits to the theater to see Sydney Poitier in *To Sir, with Love*, *The Sleep of the Prisoner*, the excellent St. John's Men's Chorus, and many more.

At this time, she began to get into golf, often going to practice her driving, and playing with a friend who was too competitive for her liking.

On the 31ˢᵗ of January, she celebrated her 59ᵗʰ birthday. She received a card from Brenda (her niece), little notes all about the apartment from Nan (her housemate) with 'Happy Birthday' on them, and a nice present of a leather-bound book "which I can use for the pictures from my trip this summer. Then, at the school, "the 4ᵗʰ form gave me a tortoise shell bracelet and pin. This was very unusual - just a class I teach. In the evening friends came and we all went over to the Trade Winds lounge, in the Paradise Island Hotel and later, the casino for an enjoyable evening."

One different experience was a visit to the opening of the Yoga Retreat. The Swami Vishnu Sevenanda started with a Hindu prayer, then Senator Isaacs declared the retreat open. "The Swami spoke and had a demonstration by his pupils. One man seemed as if he could tie himself up in knots. An Indian dancer, Mahli Ramji, gave three dances with interesting explanations. She was very good, but not my kind of dancing. After that we hastened to the Buffet. Yogis refuse meat, liquor, tobacco, coffee and tea, so it was a vegetarian buffet: rice, peas and rice, beans, lentils in a salad and cabbage salad, and a hot dish of cooked bananas. The drink was a fruit punch. The final part of the program was a bonfire on the beach. Here the Swami was to conduct a discussion. As is so usual at such things, three quarters of those present were women. I found it interesting to see people in a Christian country patronizing a heathen religion. But the Swami is said to have fifty groups all over the world. Theirs is an attempt to get away from materialism."

This is just a sample of her social life during these years. Obviously, she was not pining away in her apartment waiting for someone to share time with.

The men in Reba's life:

When I think about Reba's social life, I find myself wondering about male companionship. She had never married. Does that mean that she had no desire for male companionship or for marriage? I don't believe that was the case.

I have already mentioned that one frequent guest for several years was a man called Martin Pounder. Although Martin was 73 years of age, and Reba was just 59, she enjoyed his company and they often went around together, and if Martin had been of a mind, Reba might have considered making a life with him.

Nothing ever worked out. "A week ago, old Martin Pounder left Nassau. He has been trying to hang onto everything - the cottage and his job, but he is out. He has a marvellous trip all planned, halfway round the world and all first class. But what does he have to return to? Nothing! He has no home anywhere. For a 73-year-old, that is so pitiful. But that's the way it is when a person thinks only of one's self. He has been a very unhappy man in the past and he is going to be an unhappy man in the future."

Martin was not the only man in her life. In Ottawa lived a cousin, Geoff Miller, a scientist, a bachelor, and in many ways, a thorough bore. Since writing about the men in Reba's life, I found what I consider to be a humorous illustration of her cousin Geoff being a thorough bore. Among the books on Reba's shelves of journals, I found a hard cover book entitled *The Cryptoexplosion Structure as a Collapsed Diatrene with Hydrogen Explosions* by Geoff Miller.

This no doubt speaks of his scientific ability, while also explaining his inability to talk to Reba without talking down to her which she found irritating. Still, she spent a lot of time with him, both in Ottawa and in trips to various places. Always in the back of her mind was the question of whether Geoff would be interested in marrying her. She would have been willing. But as we shall discover later, Geoff was not the marrying kind, either.

A third man, Oliver Hunter, also figured in this period of her life. He was a very rich old man, who needed assistance, which she readily gave.

But none of these men really represented a life partner, though there is evidence that a life partner was what she longed for.

The women in Reba's life:

During her years in Nassau, Reba had a series of roommates.

One was Miss Ella Jorden, Director of the Red Cross, who moved in with Reba in January 1966. "She is so very English and sometimes in the worst way. She is definitely the old maid with all the little quirks and opinionatedness that we single women are prone to. As a companion, she is inadequate

- not a person I greatly care about. She never misses an opportunity to cut me down. I could so easily be what she is with that repulsive positiveness, that is so characteristic of the single woman. She really has an unfortunate personality. When you set yourself up as always right you at once turn others against you. She uses the Red Cross as a tool to make herself important. She is self-centred and thoroughly intolerant.

"So often those people are misfits. Ella came to Nassau filled right up with English superiority. The only way for Bahamians to act was to just let her boss them completely and set it all up in her way, the only right way. But the Bahamians did not see it that way. It's funny how these people who have lived away from England are so ultra-English, and yet deep down, they don't want to live in England. But English ways are the only right ways." In the fall, Ella left for Canada.

In September, 1968, Reba and Nan Dumbell decided to room together at a new apartment. "We have a nice view of the sea, and a swimming pool." But once again, "Nan is very anxious for a big social life and is ready to explore every avenue. The Red Cross is definitely a social thing. An outlet for wealthy and prominent people to do good works and satisfy an urge to show themselves as being philanthropic. The director spends most of her time writing invitations to this and that, bringing in well-to-do people to pack this and that for the needy because it makes these folk feel good. But so far as getting under the real needs of a place, the Red Cross doesn't have a clue.

"A week ago, tonight, Nan had her Dedication service for the Red Cross in the Cathedral. She was very thrilled and happy over it. A goodly representation of the wealthy and prominent people came and she walked down the aisle with the Governor.

"I feel Nan is in for a very unhappy time here in Nassau. Like all the other directors of the Red Cross, she belongs to an age that is past. She can't believe that these coloured people under her have rights. They must accept her as the superior English woman and they must do things her way."

Nan was indeed in for a difficult time. In the spring of 1968, she was told that she was to find a replacement for herself. She did not want to go back to England. In June, she went to a committee meeting at Government House, expecting that they would ask her to stay for another year. It did not happen and she returned home glum and weary. She did manage to stay until

December, but at last, she too was gone, and Reba says she enjoyed having the apartment to herself.

Yet, in pointing out the shortcomings in these roommates, she acknowledges that she herself had come to Nassau with her own problems.

"When I, myself, came to Nassau, I was a misfit in life, crushed and defeated by that awful thing in the Christian Church. No one helped me to find myself. In fact, so far as the GHS crowd are concerned, they no doubt poked fun behind my back at my personality problems, my oddities and gaucheries. No one was ready to take an interest in me and really help me. But I found myself by myself and I have rendered service for what I have got."

In this statement, we catch a glimpse back at the pain she endured in those final years in ministry as mentioned in Chapter Seven. There is a reference to some major difficulty with her sister in September, 1949. Wilbur and Carrie were living at that time in Dungannon, not terribly far from Varna and it appears that Wilbur may have been the chairman of the Presbytery, which made him Reba's supervisor. In another later comment she speaks of her niece Carol Ann being in her formative years and hearing negative comments from her parents at the time "when I was at my lowest ebb." Carol Ann would have been seven years old when Reba left the ministry and entered the convent.

But that painful time is behind her. She has found a new life here in Nassau, and doesn't want to dwell on the past. "I am really tired of living with misfits. I am no longer a misfit myself and I really don't enjoy being thrown in with them. I have and am learning a good lesson. I've learned to keep my mouth shut."

No doubt all of the above explains why she threw herself into such a very active social life. She compares herself to her English roommates by saying that "it is just a pure case of one person being adaptive, and another not."

Changes under the new government:

As mentioned before, 1968 was a year of change in the Bahamas as well as at Government High School. In 1967 the ruling UBP (the Bay Street Boys) had called a snap election, which the Black PLP narrowly won. As reported in *Islanders in the Stream* there followed a year when the PLP under Premier Pindling was on trial,[47] but "Premier Pindling hardly put a foot wrong."

On February 27, 1968, Premier Pindling called a general election, which he hoped would bury the UBP. The premier's optimism was justified and the PLP won a landslide victory. "The booming economy and the new political regime provided unprecedented opportunities in the public service and private sector for the black majority."

The new government began to address the inadequacy of the Bahamian educational system by making many changes. They sought to "Bahamianize the system from bottom to top.... New schools were added at the secondary level. But still they needed the expatriate teachers, mostly from Britain with some Canadians. Although these teaching imports enjoyed salaries better than their Bahamian counterparts, and more than they would have earned at home, they did not have job security. This continued reliance on expatriates was galling to many of those now in power."

Says Saunders and Craton, "Undoubtedly, the compensatory rhetoric of black power... made life difficult in the classroom and staffroom as well as outside school."[48]

Thus, not only from Reba's journals, but also from Bahamian history, it becomes evident that Reba would feel frustration with her employment at GHS She was experiencing a growing estrangement from the coloured people by this time.

In March 19, 1968, her niece, Brenda, arrived from Ontario for a visit. It is interesting to see how Reba looked forward to this visit, especially since her journal at the time of her father's death was not complimentary to this girl who had been 15 years old at that time.

Still, two years can make quite a difference and especially so, since in the meantime Reba's twin sister and Brenda's mother, Carrie, had died of cancer.

What I as her biographer had not realized until rereading her writings was that her sister Carrie had been diagnosed with cancer in 1958. Along the way, she had radiation treatments and a colostomy. At the time of their father's death in August, 1966, Carrie was not a well woman, and within a year suffered a further perforation of her bowel and died of acute peritonitis. She was

47 Craton and Saunders, *Islanders in the Stream,* p. 346
48 Ibid, p. 353.

just 59 years of age. Her daughter Carol Ann was 24 years old, while Brenda was only 16 years. How sad to lose her mother during the very years when she needed her most. Now, a few short months later, Brenda was coming to spend time with her Aunt Reba.

"I went to the airport to meet Brenda. I was really excited and wondered how Brenda would get on. She got through Customs and we were off for Nassau. She was hardly in the apartment before she began talking about her mother and how they still didn't know what had caused her death."

"Soon Brenda began talking about her father and the house. She said, 'The home is slipping badly'. She is a worried, upset, lonely girl. It is awful to think of her being left alone at her age.

"I find that Brenda is not really herself. I was amazed to find that Carol (Brenda's sister) feels the same tension with Wilbur that Brenda does."

Still, while Brenda was visiting, they spent enjoyable time together.

"Brenda and I spent the morning shopping. We had lunch at the Green Shutters. In the evening Brenda went with Brenda Knowles to a party at Gloria Smith's.

"I took the girls out for the day. We had lunch at the Coral Harbour Club. The girls swam in the pool and then I drove them about.

"I tried not to be critical of Wilbur with Brenda. Yet she is seeing that awful selfishness in him and that complete lack of consideration of others.

"Brenda and I went to Paradise Beach today. Tomorrow she leaves for Canada."

April 1, 1968: "I saw Brenda off. She was quite upset when she did her packing. She did not want to go back to Erindale.

"In May, Wilbur wrote that he had met with Carrie's doctor and had been given the report of the autopsy as I reported above."

Thus, within a couple of years of her dad's death, Reba lost her twin sister to the same kind of condition, which had taken their father's life.

"We can't speculate on what might have been. Well, the story is finished now."

Travels:

If one is unhappy with one's work, then the thought of escape into the bliss of travel becomes even more appealing.

World Traveller, Mexico

"For over a year," she writes, "I have planned to go with my cousin Louise to Europe." Reba loved to travel and so, as planned, in July she was off at last to England and Europe.

"I watched the first streaks of dawn develop into full daylight, and arrived in London where I met Louise at 8 a.m."

In reading of Reba's travels, several things are constantly in view: the quality of hotels she stayed in, the quality of the food, and the cost of everything. For much of her trip, she describes both the hotels and the food as 'poor.'

"The Picadilly Hotel included a poor continental breakfast. The service was good, the food fair only - cold toast and awful stuff called coffee. It wasn't a hotel I would choose to return to."

And so, they set off on their Europe adventure. She tells of taking a poor old ferry from Dover to Ostend - "pleasant trip but poor food - awful sausage, all bread or something - not meat and a dry piece of cake."

She describes their trip to Brussels, Belgium, through flat country, with the houses high and narrow with steeply sloping roofs. "Belgium and Holland are the two most densely populated countries in Europe."

"Through Rotterdam and Amsterdam we travelled, seeing The Hague as we went."

Amsterdam is the Netherlands' capital, known for its artistic heritage, elaborate canal system and narrow houses with gabled facades, legacies of the city's 17th-century Golden Age. Its Museum District houses the Van Gogh Museum, featuring works by Rembrandt and Vermeer at the Rijksmuseum, and modern art at the Stedelijk. Amsterdam has the reputation of being an "anything goes"[49] city. Its relaxed, permissive, tolerant, liberal approach to things like sex and drugs are legendary, so one might think there were no rules or guidelines to abide by here.

She doesn't mention the fact that one must not take pictures of the women displaying their wares in the window in the infamous Red-Light District! She does, however, give interesting information about the towns, which seem to run one town into another.

July 12: They reached the German border – "one great city after another and always the rush of traffic and great trucks."

In Cologne, in the Elite Hotel, they shared a small room, a poor communal shower and a washbasin in the room. "We arose at 5:30 and were on the bus by 7:00. We passed many gardens but always the air was smoky and, in the distance, great towns and cities. We came to Bonn, which was all badly bombed. Here was Bad-Godesborg where Chamberlain and Hitler met. At Goppard we got on a boat for a six-mile cruise down the river. The towns were charming as they nestled at the water's edge but the most interesting part were the castles."

In Heidelberg, they spent most of the time at the Heidelberg Castle, which is largely in ruins. "As we left Heidelberg, we could catch a glimpse of the Black Forest and look down into villages dotted about with white houses and red roofs. We passed Stuttgart and crossed the Danube River, which is over 2,000 miles long."

---

49 www.destinationtips.com/destinations/15-things-not-to-do-in-amsterdam

Entering Bavaria, they passed Dachow,[50] with one of the most notorious concentration camps of the last war, then Munich, Hitler's City. "It was mountainous country and very beautiful. By evening we came to Salzberg. In the morning we visited the home of Baron von Trapp and saw a fleeting glimpse of the home of Mozart."

From Salzburg they headed for Vienna, eating lunch at a lovely place in Gmunden, beside Lake Traunsee, and arriving in Vienna around 5 p.m. at the Park Hotel, which was once the guesthouse for Schonbrunn Palace.

"It was probably the best hotel we have had. In the evening we took a tour of the city to see it all illuminated, especially the Votive church. At the amusement park we took a ride on a huge Ferris wheel with about 20 of us in a hanging cage. We went to the Vienna Woods and saw the city all lighted up with the lights reflected in the Danube.

"In the morning we visited the Schonbrunn palace, the home of the Hapsburgs, a truly fabulous place with beautiful porcelain stoves in the corners of the rooms. We saw the Tapestry Room, the Chinese Room, the grand ballroom and the Millions Room, all encrusted with gold." In fact, the images of this palace online show that Reba could not even begin to describe it.

"In the evening, we went to a small opera house where a group were putting on a Rossini opera which was beautifully done. The music was lovely and so was the singing."

On July 17, they left Vienna about 8:15 a.m., driving over the Hungarian plains and up through Semmering Pass, connecting Lower Austria and Styria, between which it forms a natural border. At 4 p.m. they entered Yugoslavia where everything is owned by the state. "Our high-ceilinged room was not at all attractive. There was no bathroom, just a basin. We had a fair breakfast, and left by 9 a.m. We saw horses plowing and men and women working in the fields. The ground was not nearly as well cultivated as in the Germanic countries."

---

50 https://en.wikipedia.org/wiki/Dachau_concentration_camp
   Dachau concentration camp was the first of the Nazi concentration camps opened in Germany, intended to hold political prisoners. It is located on the grounds of an abandoned munitions factory northeast of the medieval town of Dachau, about 16 km (10 mi) northwest of Munich in the state of Bavaria, in southern Germany.

Travelling on, they stopped on top of a hill and saw Trieste below and their first sight of the Adriatic Sea. This brought them to Italy.

"We now entered Italy and came to the Largano Hotel, our stop for Venice. Here we had a gondola ride on the Grande Canal. It was a thrilling experience. The three musicians - one played a guitar and sang baritone, one played the accordion, and the third was a glorious tenor. The music floated over the water as the gondoliers lazily moved about. Venice was no disappointment. In the morning we set off for our tour of Venice by water streetcar. We stopped at St. Mark's Square where the body of St. Mark reposes. We went to the Doges' palace. We saw magnificent rooms with wonderful paintings and gloriously decorated walls. The three great painters were Titian, Tintoretto, and Veronise. We saw magnificent Titians that covered whole walls. We saw some of the dungeons and the Bridge of Sighs, where those sent to prison caught their last glimpse of freedom."

From Venice they went on to the hometown of St. Francis of Assisi, with a huge church and monastery.

Next, Umbria, and the valley of the Tiber, and thus to Sorrento with a poor hotel. In the morning they were driven to the docks through narrow winding streets where they took a boat for the Isle of Capri. From the docks they got a bus to the top of the island from which they could look down much as when we look from a plane. The view was magnificent right over the Bay of Naples.

"Coming down we saw in the distance where the Emperor Tiberius had his palace."

The next day, they left Sorrento, driving along the Bay of Naples, soon arriving at Pompeii, entering through the Marina gate. They saw many things that have been dug up including human beings who had been turned to stone by the gases of Vesuvius. The streets can be clearly seen, deeply rutted by wagon wheels.

"We had lunch at a place called Formia, then went into Rome. At first, there were vast modern apartments, then walls of the second century, which still stand. In the morning we drove to the Vatican. We saw the magnificent paintings done by Raphael and Michelangelo. At one point we could see the windows of the place where the Pope lives and saw the gardens where he walks. We went to the Sistine Chapel but it was really awful. The noise of all the guides shouting above the din to their tour groups. The ceiling is no doubt grand and the walls all beautiful paintings but one couldn't enjoy it in this atmosphere.

"After lunch, we saw the Forum which had once been the center of the city and the Coliseum which was huge. We went to the Pantheon. It is now a Christian church, then went to St. Peter's where we saw one of Michelangelo's pietas then on to the main altar. It was very thrilling to stand at the tomb of St. Peter. We saw the tombs of Pope Pius and Pope John.

"In the evening we went to the Baths of Caracalla where the Opera *Aida* was being performed. There were seats for 10,000, and we could hear easily. At the close, a chariot with two white horses dashed onto the stage. In the desert scene, in the moonlight a camel walked across the stage. It was most spectacular."

On July 25, they left the hotel at 8:45 to take a trip to the Tivoli Gardens. First, they went to the catacombs outside the city wall. There was a large underground room still used as a church. "You could still see the sign of the fish scratched on the walls." They drove 22 miles to the Tivoli Gardens where there were beautiful fountains, like an organ and like a row of candles, all done by gravity with water from the surrounding hills. As is her pattern, she describes the meals: "Our meals in Italy have been very poor – fish with the scales on, and some ground meat in a cabbage leaf. We never get a really good piece of meat."

July 26: "As we left Rome, we saw the Milvian Bridge where the Emperor Constantine saw the sign of the cross. 'By this sign conquer.' We began to see the towns built over the tops of the hills. There were vast olive groves with small olives used for oil only."

They eventually arrived at Florence and the Ambassador Hotel. No shower, only a toilet a long way down the hall.

"I was dead tired last night but managed to get to the usual horrible continental breakfast: hard rolls and poor jam and abominable coffee. We went to the top of the hill to look down over Florence, which is built all along the river Arno. Our tour ended at the church of Santa Croce where Michelangelo, Rossi, and Dante are buried."

July 28: "We left Florence, passed an old aqueduct which was well pre-served and may still be in use. We came to the famous town of Pisa, and viewed the leaning tower and now came to the Italian Riviera and to Genoa where we were shown the birthplace of Columbus. Travelling on we saw an old Roman road - the 2000-year-old Aurelian Way that once connected Rome and Spain. We crossed the border and had a view of Monaco then on to Nice, France, where we had the best hotel yet. Ruby, Louise, and I elected to go to Monaco - we walked up a long flight of steps and saw the outside of the palace of Prince Rainier. We took a bus to the Casino - wonderful paintings, frescoes and glorious ceilings, also great balconies looking out over the Mediterranean. There is nothing in the Bahamas to compare with it. I found little to interest me in the Matisse Chapel with its impressionist paint-ings, which I don't understand. Back on the bus, there were many fields of lavender, out in bloom ready for the perfume factories. We then went into the Loup Gorge. It was magnificent, with great rocky sides and with the road running along on a shelf. There was also a beautiful waterfall.

"We began to see Gourdon, perched like an eagle's nest on the top of a great mountain. It seemed quite inaccessible, but on reaching it, it is a breath-taking place."

July 31: "We left Nice and travelled through the Maritime Alps to Entrevaux which at one time was the border between Italy and France. We passed into the Haute-Savoie in the Auvergne-Rhône-Alpes region of south-eastern France, bordering both Switzerland and Italy, still very mountainous. Thus, we came to Grenoble,[51] which has one of the prettiest backdrops of any city in France as it is nestled in the Isère Valley and surrounded by inspiring mountain peaks of the French Alps."

Leaving Grenoble on August 1, they followed the Isere River and the Chartreuse Mountains, a mountain range in southeastern France, stretching from the city of Grenoble south to the Lac du Bourget north. About 10:30 they came to the border of Switzerland and on into Geneva, the headquar-ters of the Red Cross. This was French-speaking Switzerland, then into the German-speaking part. Around 6 they arrived at Lucerne and an old hotel with smelly halls.

"I am getting dreadfully tired. This is such a strenuous tour."

---

51 Grenoble, a city in the Auvergne-Rhône-Alpes region of southeastern France, sits at the foot of mountains between the Drac and Isère rivers. It's known as a base for winter sports, and for its museums, universities and research centers.

August 3. "We left Lucerne at 7 a.m. and drove along the river. It was raining and cold. We crossed a pass from the Valley of the Aar to the Valley of the Rhine and came to Basel, which is in three countries, Germany, France, and Switzerland. At 9:30 we crossed into Alsace in eastern France and came to Langres, a walled city of the 16th century and the road where Joan of Arc defeated the English."

August 4: "I will be glad when this day is over. There seems to be nothing but crowds and queues for food, and queues for the toilet. There is no doubt good food in Europe, but we don't get it."

Today, they had a tour of Paris, the Place de la Concorde, the Champs Elysees, the Arc de Triomphe and the Eifel Tower finishing at Notre Dame.

"The trouble with this tour is that there is no time to really enjoy things. In the afternoon we went to Versailles, a few miles out of Paris. In the evening we went to the Moulin Rouge. For the first time I saw girls dancing in topless costumes."

Belgium, The Netherlands, Germany, Austria, Yugoslavia, Italy, France, Switzerland. What a tour!

August 5: "I got the bus for the Orly Airport.

"At 1:30 I left Paris on a huge plane. At 3:30 Canadian time, I arrived in Montreal. Geoff and Brenda met me. We went to the Grand Hotel where we spent the night. In the morning we drove to Ottawa and were taken to the Ambassador Apartment Hotel, a real posh place where diplomats stay."

After spending time in Ottawa, Reba took the bus to Thessalon for a few days.

On her periodic visits to Thessalon and the Sault Ste. Marie area, she would enjoy time with my mother and dad, Lew and Mabel, with my brothers, Gordon and Marge, and their two boys, and with Norman and Jean and their seven children. One of them, Norm's daughter Jenat sent this comment about her memories of Reba.

From Jenat McLellan:

"As a child I was always fascinated when Reba would come visit, I remember sitting and just listening to her. Her unusual voice, the wonderful jewelry she would wear and the tales of the places she went. My wanderlust heart would so enjoy the stories. I always wanted to grow up and be exactly like her, travel to exotic places - to me they were exotic, anyways.

"The last time I remember seeing Reba was at the house in Bruce so I would have been 15 or 16. So that would be around 1975-76 or a year later 1977. But it was in my last couple years of high school. Her voice and her disposition always fascinated me. She always carried herself with such grace and one could say regal. She always wore a big beautiful gold ring with a green or red stone. But I remember it being big and beautiful. I imagined her buying it in a very exotic country. Lol. I remember always being very excited when I heard Reba was coming to visit. For some reason that I don't understand, she fascinated me. She talked about her school teaching in Nassau. I got the feeling she loved the island very much. And I loved the fact that she was her own woman. Doing what she wanted to do. A liberated personality which was uncommon and a foreign idea."

Then it was back to Toronto, where on September 9, she took the bus to Miami, and on September 15, she returned to Nassau.

On October 12, Reba resumes her regular journal.

"My summer is all over and once again I am at the old grind. I hated to start again."

On October 15, she wrote, "I think I have figured out Geoff and his ideas. He expects that when he retires, he will come to Nassau. If he marries me, it will not be until he retires. He has been deeply hurt because no one ever made anything of him in Ottawa. He thinks if he comes here, the Bahamians will be so glad to have him and bow to him when he makes common cause with them. He knows nothing about Negroes. He thinks they will make him the important man he has felt Ottawa should have made him. They wouldn't, of course. He would be as much of a misfit here, if not more than he has been in Ottawa. He feels that I should have let him know how superior he is. I haven't and that has always bothered him. He is so set in his ways and is so incapable of changing or adjusting. He thinks he is such a fine man, and that in their hearts, all his friends wish they were like him."

November 8: "In three weeks, Nan (her roommate) will be gone. How she dreads going back to England and settling in Winchester, forced to see that she is a poor woman without enough resources to live on. These people who are so 'right' and so sure of themselves, (Reba's view of those from England in general) always kill sympathy in others."

December 31, 1968: "And so I can look back over 1968. The highlight was a wonderful trip through Europe. I had a lot of good social events.

"I returned from Europe with the idea that if Geoff proposed, I would make my home in Ottawa. Geoff did not propose, and so all my ideas have gone up in smoke. In fact, I believe that he has no intention of making a home in Ottawa."

Once again, as her biographer, I am struck by her longing for the stability of a home and a husband.

No, Reba, there is no marriage in sight for you. In fact, your time in Nassau is not at an end, so you should be prepared for more concerns about Nassau.

CHAPTER TWELVE

More Concerns about Nassau

"Human progress is neither automatic nor inevitable....
Every step toward the goal of justice requires sacrifice,
suffering, and struggle; the tireless exertions and
passionate concern of dedicated individuals."

— Martin Luther King Junior

As Nassau entered 1969, Reba continued to express her concerns, not openly or publicly, but privately in her journal.

She included a column from the *Tribune* newspaper, February 1, 1969, by Chick Charney, about a mass meeting of the teachers in which it was revealed that the Ministry of Education planned to spend $14½ million dollars on putting carpets in all of the schools, while ignoring the complaint that teachers were lacking the necessary books and supplies to help them teach effectively. Writes the reporter, "There is no excuse for these facts to be unknown to the Acting Director of Education who was a former teacher. Teachers wanted to know why they could never reach anyone when they called the Ministry. Others wanted to know why they were never consulted."

Reba states that the Acting Director of Education was Lew Morgan. "In my view, Lew and a lot of these teachers from England just aren't able for positions of importance."

She wondered what Lew's real job is since over him were a minister, a permanent secretary, and a director. "Where does he stand? He will simply be the handy man for all the rest."

This comment shows that Reba's concerns were not limited to the black leadership but extended also to expatriates from England. Of course, she had already shown her feelings about people from England expecting to be made much of in Nassau, which did not happen.

"There is no sense of service and no devotion anywhere. This awful selfishness and greed has seeped into the whole of life here, and no one can help now. And the churches are all the same. They are as dead as the boards and cement they are made of."

Always the observer, in March, she includes a column by Etienne Dupuch, Editor of the *Tribune*. The editor states that, "It is really difficult to be an idealist in this country. I am afraid that they must be taught the hard way. The magic city of Freeport (the developing area of rapid expansion) is haunted by frustration, disillusionment, and fear… on the part of those who have sunk all their savings into this boomtown. I am told on every hand of people who have sold out and left."

Because of her concerns, Reba began moving money from her bank in Nassau to Canada.

"At the bank today, I wondered about transferring the $3,000 in my savings account to Canada. The accountant was called, and my account was signed to send to Canada on Monday morning. From the secretary and accountant, I got the feeling that the matter was urgent and I shouldn't wait. When the crash comes it will come fast. The school is doomed. The time is too late now, and the country is doomed too."

Of course, the banks did not collapse and the school did not collapse either, but the situation was serious enough that Craton and Saunders wrote about it: 'Honeymoon over: Depression and Discord, '1970-1973'.[52]

"Statements of moderate principles and intentions were all very well, but they could not in themselves restore investors' confidence, any more than they could reverse the downward trend in the world economy that began in 1969… the early 1970's were a period of economic and political crisis for the Bahamas as a whole."

Tourism had fallen off, Bahamas Airways collapsed on October 9, 1970, and the Bahamas Christian Council urged Bahamians to avoid the casinos, which were "inherently demoralizing, offering illusory promises of unearned wealth and temptations of corruption."

---

52 Craton and Saunders, *Islanders in the Stream*, p. 355 - 358.

Internal difficulties damaging to the PLP came about when Cecil Wallace-Whitfield and seven other members left the party and formed a new party called The Free National Movement (FNM), which became the new official opposition.

From all these concerns, Reba welcomed time away. She spent a weekend on Cat Island. She had heard that conditions were very primitive and that is what she found. In spite of the fact that the Hawk's Nest Club, which she visited, had the best of everything, the people on the island still lived as their grandparents did in small stone houses, roofed with thatch, with no running water and no electricity. However, for a population of 3,000 people, there were numerous churches of every denomination.

Back in Nassau, school ended and it was time for another trip - an extensive tour of Great Britain.

On July 5, she flew from Nassau to Bermuda where she spent three days with friends.

"My impressions: Bermuda is a wee island, 600 miles from any land. It has many inlets and is hilly but with no high hills. Its houses are practically all made of concrete with roofs made of slabs of native stone, put together with plaster and concrete and ridges so that all water runs into a cistern. There is no water on Bermuda at all so all water for drinking and domestic use must come from a cistern. As a result, you don't flush the toilet every time and you don't have a bath every day.

"It is a clean and attractive island with coloured people with a strong Indian blend, whose houses are mostly as good as the whites. It has no rural area as it is nearly all built up. It is attractive but I would never want to live there."

On July 8, after an all-night flight, she arrived in London where she met Nan Dumbell, her former roommate, who was now living in Winchester, southwest of London, not far from the English Channel. She found the 54-degree Fahrenheit weather a welcome change after the 90 degrees in Nassau.

A few days in London were spent shopping at Harrods, and seeing a couple of plays: *Forty Years On* with (Sir) John Gielgud, and *She Stoops to Conquer* at the Garrick Theatre.

I find it interesting that, having been glad to see Nan leave Nassau, she now enjoyed spending time with her and visiting Nan's friends and relatives. Having never been to England, myself, like many of my readers, I can only vicariously appreciate the places they visited on this tour.

On the 20th, they drove through surrounding towns and to Stonehenge.

"Stonehenge was standing on a rise of ground with a wide plane all around. It was beautifully planned. I was surprised at how small Stonehenge was. We went back through some quaint villages, one in particular, Broughton, where we went into an old church dating from 1080."

On July 21, she and her fellow teacher, Margaret Hyslop, and Margaret's mother, Mrs. Hyslop, started off for Scotland.

"Our first stop was Oxford which we reached in the early evening. Oxford, with its prestigious university, is made up of 38 Colleges. I took a walk through Exeter College. There was an old and striking tapestry in its chapel.

"We found a bed and breakfast at the St. Giles Hotel for 2.40 lb. ($5.30). We had a room on the very top overlooking a compound of Regent College. We went out to dinner at Golden Cross, all in the courtyard of an old stage-coach Inn. The food was only fair."

They spent the 22nd in Oxford – seeing the Martyr's Cross near the place where Cranmer and Ridley were burned. They went into Balliol College, the Scottish College. From there they went through Trinity and into the Bodleian library. She says, "The things that interested me were 1) a letter written by a boy of Alexandra to his family on papyrus. 2) letters written by Charles II and Charles I and a very smug letter by Bernard Shaw. The writing of Charles was so peculiar it was hard to read."

They next went to the Sheldonian Theatre, which is used for the graduation ceremonies of Oxford. "It has a beautiful and ornate ceiling, unusual because it is flat. Our lunch was at a place called Littlewoods. In the afternoon we viewed 3 colleges: Magdalen, which had a cloister and a deer park, built along the river Cherwell. There is a grand walk all along the river. We next visited Oriel, which had a rounded and interesting entrance. We viewed the Great Hall. Our last college was Christchurch. It is the largest college and has a huge square and an immense Great Hall quite evidently in constant use. The Cathedral had a very interesting medieval window. It has the striking blues which I associate with medieval. We then went back to the hotel. Mrs.

Hyslop had been sitting in the park for the afternoon. We had an excellent meal in very attractive surroundings at the Roebuck."

In the days after, they explored other attractive sites before driving through the Midlands.

"We stopped at a small place called Hunley where there was a castle which dates away back but has constantly been lived in. We stayed at the Castle Hotel, which was a poor place –very old and musty.

"There was a little river here which flowed into the Lune and I discovered that people pay shocking prices for fishing rights along stretches of the river as the Lune has salmon in it."

They then travelled through the Lake District and entered Scotland.

"We crossed the border into Scotland at Gretna and drove on to Dumfries. Here we were taken by Margaret to the Waverly Hotel. These are a poor grade of hotels that Margaret and her mother go to."

In the afternoon they went for a drive past Alvaston Farm, which had once been worked by Robbie Burns. They saw the castle where Margaret's grandfather once farmed.

"We then drove to Margaret's old auntie's place. It was very old fashioned and reminded me of the farmhouses of Mother's Day in Algoma.

"We had a Scottish tea with three kinds of scones and delicious rhubarb jam. The auntie came with us and we drove to the house where Annie Laurie lived. I was surprised to see how big it was. This is all well settled country. There are plenty of small houses but plenty of large ones as well."

On July 27, Margaret drove her to the bus depot where she booked a bus ticket, for she felt that she must see Scotland.

"I set off in a double decker bus for Glasgow. We passed through Ayr and the Burns' country and in the middle of the afternoon arrived in Glasgow, a drab, dreary bus station with no facilities."

One thing that always was true of my cousin – she was completely comfortable travelling by herself, whatever the mode of transportation.

From Glasgow, she took a bus to Fort William.

"Leaving Glasgow with its fantastic population all massed on top of one another before long, we were driving along Loch Lomond. Then the grass-covered mountains began to appear.

"It is a very beautiful road as we drove on into the mountains.

"Above the tree line, the heather is so short. It wasn't quite out. The mountains are covered with grass and few trees. There were scattered flocks of sheep but few houses or crofts as they call them.

"We came to a very bleak country, then into the eerie Glen Coe where an awful massacre took place - a deep glen in great high bleak mountains. We came out to Loch Linnhe with Fort William on its banks."

Fort William is a town in the western Scottish Highlands, on the shores of Loch Linnhe. It's known as a gateway to Ben Nevis, the U.K.'s highest peak, and Glen Nevis valley, home to Steall Falls. The nearby Nevis Range Mountain Resort has ski runs and forest trails.

"The traffic in Fort William was awful. The place was jammed with tourists. You could hardly walk on the streets they were so crowded. Accommodation in any of the hotels was impossible.

"We travelled along Loch Lochy, the Caledonian Canal, and Loch Ness. It was a lovely drive. We passed the Castle Urquhart, where the Loch Ness monster is supposed to come up and sun himself."

She next travelled northeast to Inverness, almost to the Moray Firth. As I look at a map of the British Isles, the Moray Firth is a deep triangular inlet from the North Sea, which cuts diagonally through Scotland causing the top part of Scotland to look remarkably like a cock's comb, the fleshy appendage on a rooster's head.

She finally found a room in a private home but she learned a bitter lesson: Never travel in Scotland without accommodation.

She next went back to Fort William where she boarded the George V for a trip to the Island of Iona. They were ferried to the shore by smaller boats. "It is a bleak place of grass- covered hills and threatening sea. Conferences of people come here for meditation and prayer but there is no permanent habitation. Some of Scotland's kings are buried here."

On July 31, "We travelled today by bus to Edinburgh, passing through some of Scotland's highest mountains.

"When I arrived in Edinburgh, I was taken to the Carlton Hotel where I had a lovely room and bath. It just seemed wonderful. Then I had dinner served very well in a beautifully well-appointed dining room."

August 1: "In the afternoon I took a tour of the city. First to St. Giles Cathedral, a beautiful building which is the tomb of the Duke of Argyll and the Duke of Montrose. Saw a window depicting John Knox preaching. He was the first minister of St. Giles. From St. Giles, we went to Holyrood Palace. Here we saw the bedrooms of Mary, Queen of Scots, and Lord Darnley. We saw the crown jewels and the audience room of Mary and Lord Darnley. We saw the little room where James I of England and James VI of Scotland were born. What I liked the best was the chapel of Queen Margaret. She was the wife of Malcolm III. She was very religious and a woman I would like to learn more of.

"On August 3, we travelled back into England and made our way once again to Winchester where Nan lives. Nan and I are going to travel through Ireland. I am looking forward to it."

August 5: "We rose early and a taxi drove us to the airport where we boarded a plane for Ireland. I was much interested in seeing the Isle of Mann from the air. Between 10 and 11 we landed at the Belfast airport. We drove northeast to Larne and then along the northern coast. I was thrilled by the rocky headlands and beauty of the coast."

In their travels through Northern Ireland, they drove past Port Rush, through Coleraine and Limavady and past Londonderry.[53] At the border, there was merely a formality and they drove into the Republic of Eire and the County of Donegal.

She describes their trip through Eire, to one of the stops that she wanted to make.

"At Ballina, we left the coast and drove to Baleel and then into Fermanagh in Northern Ireland. I was deeply touched on coming to the county where Grandpa Stinson was born and lived until he was 21. Good rolling farmland. Lough Erne was lovely. It is full of islands."

On they went through towns and villages, "We left Galway and drove on around the coast. There are many evidences of the past in Ireland - ruined abbeys and castles. From Bunrally, we drove on to Tralee and to a most excellent hotel - the Mount Branden. We had a room and bath and the food and dining room was first class."

---

53 Tralee is a town in County Kerry, in southwestern Ireland. It's known for the Rose of Tralee International Festival. https://en.wikipedia.org/wiki/Tralee

Does not the word of her travels through Ireland bring to mind some of those songs of Ireland you have sung since childhood? "My Wild Irish Rose"; "The Rose of Tralee"; "Oh, Danny Boy"; "When Irish Eyes are Smiling".

They kept bearing south to Blarney Castle, a beautiful place. She describes it as a lovely park of great trees and a river flowing through. The castle is quite well preserved. "We had many narrow curving steps to climb and many people doing the same. The Blarney stone is at the very top and you have to lie on your back and cross a deep narrow chasm to kiss it. Your legs are held by an attendant. I didn't kiss it."

On August 15, they hurried on to the airport and got there just in time for their plane. They got to Eastleigh[54] and returned to Winchester where their trip began.

Next, she planned a trip through Wales and Cornwall.

On August 21, she took the train from Winchester to London. From the Waterloo Station she took a taxi to Euston and left for Chester coming up through the Midlands. Nearly all the way was along canals. Once these were used for horse-drawn freight barges, but that is all gone now and only holidaymakers have boats on the canals.

"I took a taxi to the bus stop for Llangollenin Wales. A very nice girl carried my suitcase to the reception desk at the Royal Hotel. It is a lovely hotel situated on the River Dee. I was given a single room with a private bathroom. I had a sandwich and coffee sitting in a big bay window in the lounge with the river running swiftly over rapids just outside the window and in full view.

"In the morning I went to a Methodist Church on the river. A lovely setting. It was a very well-kept-up church and nicely appointed. It would hold I suppose 150. If there were 25 present that was all. The minister was an old man playing the pipe organ. It was cold and unfriendly. I felt as if I had wasted my time."

As I write this, I take note of the fact that, in spite of all Reba's mixed feelings about churches and denominations, she continued to seek out a church on Sundays, often only to be disappointed again.

---

54 Eastleigh is in Hampshire, England. The town lies between Southampton and Winchester.

It is also interesting because this week, I am burying a man from Wales. This has led me to read about the great revivals in Wales, particularly in 1859 and 1904. During those revivals, thousands of people were brought into a personal relationship with Christ, filling the churches and causing new churches and chapels to be started. Between those revivals and afterward, the fire of spiritual zeal gradually died down. My friend Tom Jones[55] and his family were part of one of those churches. His brother was a minister in their home church, and after Tom came to Canada to be near his daughter and son-in-law, he continued to send money home to that church. Unfortunately, that church is like this one, which Reba visited, with few people in attendance, just struggling to survive.

My sermon for Tom's funeral reminds us all that, "God has no grandchildren!" John 1: 11-13: "He (Jesus) came unto his own, and his own received him not. But as many as received him, to them gave he power to become the sons of God, even to them that believe on his name: Which were born, not of blood, nor of the will of the flesh, nor of the will of man, but of God."

No one is a Christian because his father or grandfather was a Christian. When people start living on memories of God's work rather than personally entering into a relationship with God, the results will always result in empty churches, and empty hearts. Such is the case in Wales.

One lingering remnant of the great revivals is found in Wales being known as "The Land of Song." Throughout the land, men began to break into song, into hymns with delightful harmonies. This continues to this day, so that I read that, "Singing is a significant part of Welsh national identity, and the country is traditionally referred to as "the land of song". This is a modern stereotype based on 19th century conceptions of Nonconformist choral music and 20th century male voice choirs."

Reba describes travelling through beautiful mountains and seeing waterfalls. "Altogether," she says, "it was a lovely trip. It was about 7 p.m. when we got back to Llangollen."

Her trip continued on through Wales, arriving in Tenby and the Royal Gatehouse Hotel. "The service in the dining room was superb and the food good. It is a good hotel though with no private bathroom.

---

55 Permission given by Gloria Bench, daughter, March 14, 2019.

"On August 31, we passed through the big city of Bristol and into Summerset and to the Manley's hills. I have now left Wales. I had an excellent dinner at the County, one of the best I have had."

South to Plymouth, to Exeter,[56] and into Devon, which is pretty rolling farm country.

I pick up my ears as I read of passing through Devonshire, because that is where our Hern forebears come from. My dad seemed to feel that we had a Welsh background, but I have traced my great grandfather and his family back to Devonshire, so my cousin was travelling in family country. She does not mention meeting any Herns but there were many of them there.

"We saw the river Dart and passed along the edge of Dartmoor. I walked to the seaside and the promenade. It was very interesting to stand on the hill where they first saw the Armada coming.

"We arrived in Penzance[57] at 7. I got a taxi and came to the Queen's Hotel, another good one. You can see St. Michael's Mount quite clearly. Had a good dinner in a beautiful dining room with a lovely view of the sea and the headland."

September 3: "I booked a tour. On this tour, I had an old gentleman sitting beside me this trip and he was good company. This was a good day and I really felt that I would enjoy having a bathing suit on. The water was a beautiful blue and looked very inviting. The coast of Cornwall is certainly lovely. I very much enjoyed the day."

Soon Reba came back to her friend Nan's place in Winchester from which she had started out on her tour of the whole of Great Britain and Ireland. But she was not done yet.

---

56 Exeter is a cathedral city in Devon, England, with a population of 129,800 (mid-2016 est.). The city is on the River Exe about 37 miles (60 km) northeast of Plymouth and 70 miles (110 km) southwest of Bristol. It is the county town of Devon.

57 Penzance is a town, civil parish and port in Cornwall, in England, United Kingdom. It is the most westerly major town in Cornwall and is about 75 miles (121 km) west of Plymouth and 300 miles (480 km) west-southwest of London. Situated in the shelter of Mount's Bay, the town faces south-east onto the English Channel.

On September 5, "At 12:30 Nan and I left in her car for Southampton and the Isle of Wight. [58]

"We went by ferry down the Southampton water and arrived at East Cowes.

"Osborne House was a residence of Queen Victoria. It is not a pretty house and not very wonderful. It was filled with the presents given by the Rajahs and Princess of India to the various monarchs of England especially Victoria. It all represents a day now gone and it was noticeable how prominent were the men of great wealth in India. There were many pictures of them. England's real contact with India was with these and not with the common people.

"From there we drove inland to Vendun and Bonchurch where we called in at the Peacock Vane. There was only the housekeeper to greet us but it is all very posh and high and mighty. We had a drink in the lounge and then went to the cottage where we had a lovely double room with a big bay window and a 3-piece bathroom. There is also a pleasant little sitting room for all the guests in the cottage.

"Dinner was at 8 o'clock. Dinner was terribly expensive even for England. I had soup, and macaroni both very ordinary, then we had chateaubriand steak. It was excellent but not generous and there were a lot of vegetables. The dessert was on a sweet wagon and you chose what you wanted. It was no doubt a good dinner but I didn't enjoy it nearly as much as I did the dinner at the County Hotel at Taunton, which was half the price.

"The day after tomorrow I leave for Nassau. I have had a good view of the U.K. and will not be wanting to return for some time."

September 10: "In the morning we drove into Portsmouth to see the ship *Victory*, Nelson's flag ship. I felt thrilled at first sight of it with its rows of guns, it looked very formidable indeed. A sailor met our party and took us on board. He showed us Nelson's sleeping quarters between the guns. His fancy

---

58   The Isle of Wight is an island off the south coast of England. It's known for its beaches and seafront promenades such as sandy Shanklin Beach and south-facing Ventnor Beach, which is dotted with vintage beach huts. Dinosaur remains and fossils can be seen in areas like Compton Bay and Yaverland Beach. On the island's western point, The Needles are three huge, white chalk rocks, guarded by a 19th-century lighthouse.
https://en.wikipedia.org/wiki/Isle_of_Wight

little hammock looked so small. He was only 5 feet, 1 inch tall. We saw his dining hall and living room. We then went below to the deck. Here we saw the vast gun deck and sailor's hammocks slung with 20 inches for each one."

As her biographer, I am sure that we can all identify with her in this experience. Our history lessons tended to glorify the red-coated British soldiers at the Plains of Abraham and many other victories. But now Reba sees a different side of Army and Navy life of the British. "We saw the awful instrument of flogging and were given a vivid description of it. Often the man died. His back would be cut to the bone. What fantastic cruelty. On these lower decks we saw where the men ate. Wooden tubs - one for stew, one for water, one for spirits and one for wine.

"They had no dishes or cutlery for they ate with their hands and had one meal a day which was always stew. The tables were fitted between the guns. 14 men ate at a table with a boy to wait on them sitting at the end. These lower decks were all dreadfully low and we learned that the average height of the men was 5 feet, 2 or 3 inches. There seemed to be no means of washing and the squalor must have been awful. On one deck lived 400 men and all these men were pressed into the Navy. When I remarked on this, Neville answered, "Who would volunteer for this?"

"All the thrill and all the romance of the Victory left me now for a feeling of revulsion. When England was building her Empire, what awful cruelty she used."

I am sure that she now began to look somewhat differently upon the Bahamas' struggle for independence.

September 11: "I had lunch with Nan around 11 and they got ready and she drove me to the station to catch the train to London and went to the BOAC Air Terminal. At 4:30 the plane was loaded and soon took off.

"We were served afternoon tea. It took 7 hours to get to Bermuda. We put our watches back 5 hours. As the plane was late, we just had 20 minutes. In another 2 hours I was in Nassau. Martin was at the airport to meet me. And so, my summer holidays came to an end.

"There are one or two observations I want to make.

"I have now had a good look at the U.K. so I don't need to return there. It has many sweet things to offer, but there are far too many people. Every sight you see is so crowded with people it is awful.

"So far as Nan is concerned. I had a pleasant time with her and she was most kind. Yet I know she could never be a close and dear friend to me."

Back in Nassau:

September 26: "I have been two weeks back at GHS The deterioration that has been going on has at last become public. There were only 39.4% passes - the poorest of any of the high schools in the colony."

At GHS, Reba states, "I have lost all faith in the Ministry of Education. The Acting Headmaster now is Alwyn David, who won't stand up for his teachers, and blames the failing grades in English on the quality of the students. When I brought to his attention the poor English results, his reply was, 'Oh, but these students – what can you expect?' But there's no one any better.

"As I prayed tonight, I realized that what has happened to GHS, was inevitable. When they accepted children of the shacks on the same basis as those of good homes, the trouble started. I suppose they thought that they would elevate the shack children. Instead, the shack children dragged the school down to their level."

She reports that the school inspector is to speak to the students on Friday but she says that he has the horrible attitude of the English, full of contempt for anything Bahamian. In turn, she can see all the nasty attitudes among the children toward the staff. Surely in all of this we see Reba's own response and understanding of Bahamian attitudes to colonial repression.

Of the government, she believes that they have made a mess of things. Her fellow teacher, Evelyn Knowles, has been advised by her lawyer to get her money out of Nassau, and make sure of her Canadian citizenship but she won't take his advice. People in the hairdressing shop are claiming that there will be a collapse within six months.

Though she was upset with the school, she continued to do her job. In November, she tells of marking essays, one of which was "a real doozy". One of the students gave graphic details of a wild evening, involving picking up girls. She did not report this to the headmaster as he would do nothing, so she chose to ignore it.

"The time has come for expatriates to get out."

Of course, she did not get out. Not till July, 1974.

As I read this part of Reba's story, I feel deeply saddened. It is obvious that she is thoroughly disillusioned. As in her former times of stress, her problems arise from being caught in a time of major change through no fault of her own. It probably would have been good if she could have returned home to Canada, but, like other expatriates of whom she has written, there was nothing waiting for her here, so instead she must try to adjust to the changing conditions in her adopted country.

As we see her distress with the conditions at GHS, I wonder how often her mind went back to the painfulness of her later ministry years, which we reported in Chapter 7.

Is she now to see a repeat of the sorrows of those past days? It's time to get away again, even if it involves "A Strange Companionship."

Chapter Thirteen

A Strange Companionship

"Those who have never known the deep intimacy and the intense companionship of happy mutual love have missed the best thing that life has to give."

— Bertrand Russell

As she entered 1970, Reba's journals become less centered on the situation at Government High School and more on her personal life.

Under the new black government, Nassau was changing from dependence on British sterling currency to the Bahamian dollar. It was building new schools at a time when there were too few qualified Bahamian teachers, while seeking to 'Bahamianize' the educational system.

Meanwhile, she had a third housemate in a row from England. Once again, Barbara Rushmer was not a very satisfactory companion. Reba describes her as "a highly excitable woman who gets tiresome when one has her all the time."

It makes me wonder how she kept accepting these English women as roommates, when each of them exhibit similar tendencies.

Barbara and her husband 'Rush' had sold their house and given up their jobs in England and decided to make their home in Nassau. Reba says that they had all the ideas of the superior English person coming to the colonies.

Barbara was teaching at the Deaf Centre. Tongue firmly in cheek, Reba states that,

"The little deaf children and the people of Nassau would be filled with gratitude to this wonderful English couple who were doing them such a great service. Of course, the children would not be up to the standard of English children, but their humble thanks would make up for their lack."

Says Reba, "I can hardly keep from roaring with laughter as I write this. What a shock Barbara got! She is so desperately typical of the English teachers who come to Nassau. If she had had common sense, she would have realized that Bahamian people, especially since the victory of the PLP government in 1968, and the movement toward independence, were being set free from the sense that they were entirely dependent on the English for everything."

Meanwhile, Barbara's husband Rush decided that he would get into the charter boat business. With no research into the matter and with seemingly little thought for his wife, who was finding that these little deaf children were not the delightful urchins she had imagined, he set off for England to buy a boat, leaving her without even necessary funds to buy a used car.

We understand why Reba was glad to get away from this whole situation on a spring break trip with her cousin Geoff from Ottawa.

On March 26, 1970, Reba flew to New Orleans, Louisiana, then on to San Antonio, Texas. Geoff was at the airport to meet her. In the morning, they set off to see San Antonio.

"We parked the car and walked, visiting an old mission. We walked along the San Antonio River. San Antonio is on a flat plain, a city of small wooden houses.

"I was very interested in the flat country on which the forces of Gen. Santa Anna had come as they prepared to attack the brave Texans. The really thrilling sight was the Alamo itself - the old church is a museum with pictures of the battle and of its leading men."

They drove through Texas, including a visit to Big Bend National Park. They saw the magnificent Santa Elena Canyon on the Rio Grande.

"We took a good walk along the canyon wall, which had no guardrail and was very narrow with a great drop to the river. The other side of the canyon was Mexico. The Rio Grande in not really a big river at this point. It is in no way commercialized, just natural."

March 30: "Yesterday was Easter Sunday but we didn't get to church. We left the mountains and drove over the great plains of Texas with so much mesquite. The roadside was covered with flowers."

They came into country that is famous in stories of the Wild West: 'West of the Pecos.'

"There were no houses - just mesquite for miles. We passed the town of Langtree as it sits on the steep canyon of the Rio Grande. Came to the Pecos River, which runs in a deep canyon. The Canyon walls are almost straight up and down. We could see where the Pecos and the Rio Grande joined.

"We saw a beautiful cactus in bloom. We came to Del Rio on the border. There were many Mexicans. Drove along the Rio Grande to Eagle Pass and along the border of Mexico. I longed to go into Mexico but Geoff has no passport. The Canyon walls are almost straight up and down. At the Pecos, we could see where the Pecos and the Rio Grande joined. We drove down to Laredo where we stayed at The Sands Motel - fair. We had a Mexican dinner. Guacamole, tamales, mashed beans, Spanish rice, taco, and one half hot green pepper. It was o.k."

Here, she relates an interesting experience, which would suggest that she might have accepted some romantic attention from Geoff, but Geoff simply went off to his own bedroom. They spent a good part of a day at Aransas Wildlife Reserve where they saw lovely azaleas and wisteria, and had a grand view of whooping cranes. She reports that there are only about 56 of them left outside of captivity. It was a great treat to see them. They also saw pelicans, a wild turkey, many deer, an armadillo, and two alligators.

"We spent the night at Galveston. Geoff decided we would have dinner at a big posh hotel. We had a lovely dinner of fried oysters served in a very good dining room.

"This is all oil country with many refineries. We stopped for lunch at the border of Texas and Louisiana. We were now in the land of big live oaks hanging with Spanish moss."

On April 3, they travelled across Louisiana, and down the delta of the Mississippi where they saw the shrimp fleet and stayed at Lockport. It was interesting for them to hear the shrimp fishermen talking. "Most are Cajun and talk French with southern drawl."

"Before we left New Iberia, I was determined that I must see at least one antebellum mansion."

Now that is a word which I do not know so I had to look it up: "Antebellum architecture (meaning "prewar", from the Latin *ante*, "before", and *bellum*, "war") is the neoclassical architectural style characteristic of the 19th-century Southern United States, especially the Deep South, from after the birth of the United States with the American Revolution, to the start of the American Civil War. Antebellum architecture is especially characterized by Georgian, Neo-classical, and Greek Revival style plantation homes and mansions."[59]

"A short distance out we came to Albania and I insisted in going in even if Geoff was not interested. It was beautifully kept up and one could easily see how the rich of Louisiana lived before the war of 1865. This house had been owned by a Frenchman. I was interested in the bedrooms. In the entrance to each was a small hall with two small rooms on each side. One was a room for bathing and dressing, the other a room for clothes. The furniture inside was all antique. One could easily imagine the women in their crinolines walking over the lawns. We then drove to the Rip Van Winkle Gardens and spent a long time walking about.

"We drove on to New Orleans. In the evening we went to the French Quarter. It would have been fun to have gone to a gay (prior to the change of meaning of this word) nite spot. But poor old Geoff doesn't know they exist. I had to be satisfied with an expensive good dinner in Le Vieux Carre. I had wine but Geoff declined. Geoff believes he is being a very good, fine person of highest moral principle by acting as he does. He doesn't realize that only his mama and a few old folks of another day understand it that way. The rest look upon him as square and a dull, uninteresting person. Does he think he is making a sacrifice for righteousness' sake, but if so, to what purpose? He is not religious. When we had dined, we went back to the motel - no nite life for us."

April 5: "In the morning we took a drive along the Mississippi. Our trip was finished. At 1:30 I went to the airport and about 2:30 flew to Miami and Nassau. Barbara met me at the airport."

Back in Nassau:

April 6: "Yesterday I returned from a trip through Texas and Louisiana with Geoff. I went, wondering if Geoff would propose to me, but once again, he didn't. I know now he has no intention of doing so. I am a companion to take the place of his mother. Three times on this trip he actually called me 'mother'. He has lived too long alone. He could never adjust to living

---

59 https://en.wikipedia.org/wiki/Antebellum_architecture

with anybody. One can never have a nice chatty conversation with him. He wants to lecture you on whooping cranes, or roadrunners, but he never wants you to lecture him. If I would start to talk about something, he would inevitably break in with, 'Oh, come, come,' and proceed to show me as being inconsistent, by quoting from a letter something that I had said. He wants to gain status by reducing me. He can't sit and chat with anyone in mutual conversation. As a result, he remains one of life's misfits, friendless and alone. Like Rush, with Barbara, he lived in his own little world, oblivious to my wants or needs."

We have seen already that if Geoff had offered to marry her, she would have been willing to make a home with him, but this was not Geoff. Truly, Geoff and Reba had a strange companionship. Thank goodness it never amounted to something that she might have regretted for the rest of her life.

As Reba arrived back in Nassau, her activities resumed. 'Rush' Rushmer arrived with his boat, after his trip across the Atlantic from England and they had a party for him. Once more, we hear of a round of parties, golfing, and other activities.

Her very brief journal entries tell of various parties and social events plus her weekly attendance at Trinity Methodist Church.

"I went to a small barbeque dinner party. Played 18 holes of golf - badly."

April 29: "After school I had a Red Cross meeting." She seems, at this point, to personally be more involved with the Red Cross.

June 26: "The last day of school. I took 8 Junior Red Cross members and 4 welfare children to Paradise Island for picnic, but it was not really a very successful venture."

June 27, 1970: "Yesterday the school once again broke up for the summer. How I wish I was all finished with GHS but I have been wishing that for a number of years now.

"Each year the school goes down a little further. Al David has not the dignity of a head, nor the respect of the students, so there is a slackness and contempt for authority. Even Evelyn has to accept that 6th form students walk out of her classes because they think what she is teaching is not relevant. The students are also ignoring Margaret Thomas, another of their teachers, because they believe she is old-fashioned and outmoded. Actually, they are 100% right. She has no real understanding of the students or their needs. She is completely incapable of changing with the times nor with the students of the Bahamas."

More travels: to Ontario, Alberta, and the Yukon:

With school finished, Reba flew for another time to Toronto. Geoff was at the airport to meet her.

Two days after she arrived, she wrote, "Today, I returned to the Catholic Church, made confession at St. Michael's Cathedral and took communion." Two days later: she again went to Mass and took communion.

I find it interesting to watch her continuing attempts to find meaning in her religious life.

Is anything really satisfying her soul at this stage of her life?

Once again, she spent the weekend at Bramalea with her brother-in-law, Wilbur Rogers. She bought her tickets to go to Thessalon to visit with my family, and for her trip to British Columbia. There are no notes for this part of her trip.

On July 26, she visited her cousin Louise in northern Alberta. Her notes briefly tell of her visit in Grand Centre, "a typical western town noticeably colder than Algoma. Temperature 63 degrees in the day and 50 degrees at night." For the few days she was there the weather remained wet and cold. Dull days in a northern Alberta farm town.

"One afternoon Louise had a tea for me with about 10 women. Then we drove out to see the R.C.A.F base of Cold Lake. It is a large town, but with all same type of houses."

She stayed a couple more days, and saw the movie *The Love Bug* which was very entertaining, a real comedy, but she wondered if Louise was really enjoying having her.

From Grande Centre, her bus carried her through Bonnyville, St. Paul, Vilna, and Smoky Hole to Edmonton. "Many mountains had snow on top. We drove toward a glorious sunset in the Rockies. The road is gravel and very dusty. A magnificent day. We drove on to midnight as I was on that bus all night. It got dark about 11 p.m." This, of course is very typical of life this far north. In summer it is light nearly all night – almost an extended twilight.

August 7, 1970: "Today, started very early as I was watching for the dawn. We passed Teslin Lake. Teslin Lake is a large lake spanning the border between British Columbia and Yukon, Canada. It is one of a group of large lakes in the region of far northwestern BC. These lakes are known in Yukon as "the Southern Lakes" and are the headwaters of the Yukon River itself.

"Beautiful scenery. We arrived in Whitehorse then left for a wonderful drive to Dawson City. There were few on bus, no towns nor farms. I had good company on the bus - Joe Pacquin and a Public Health nurse. In Dawson, I went to the Robert Service Motel."

After a day like that and a night with little or no sleep, I am surprised that Reba can navigate. But we have discovered before that she is a tough woman with lots of stamina. We'll see that again in some of her later trips where it is a wonder that she could keep on going. Another evidence of her robust constitution: there never seems to be an extra trip or tour that she is not eager to go on.

"We saw the Klondike today. A lovely fast river, then the place of the mine's vast mountains of tailings - nearly as much earth moved here as the St. Lawrence Seaway. We came to Bonanza Creek with tailings all up the gorge. We next viewed the place where the Klondike and Yukon Rivers meet. The Yukon has silt but the Klondike is clear.

"40,000 people once lived in Dawson, but now there are only 40,000 in all the Yukon."

August 8 was a wet day. She heard some Americans in the dining room saying, "I thought all Canadians would speak with an English accent, but they don't. In the east they speak French."

August 9: "In the morning I attended St. Mary's church, then went for a walk. I saw Ruby Scott's, a madam's house. In the afternoon, I went to the gold fields, Bonanza and Eldorado and panned for gold. I had supper at the Midnight Sun and had a grand talk with a bush pilot." Reba would resonate with northerners in the Yukon. They would embrace her independence and self-sufficiency.

On August 10, she met Bessie, an old friend from Algoma. Together, they went to the Midnight Dome with its glorious view. It is said no trip to Dawson is complete without capturing a photograph of yourself atop the Midnight Dome where you may take in a panoramic view of the region and marvel in the beauty of the Yukon River and Klondike Valleys. You may also spy on the Ogilvie Mountain Range in the distance. A tour of the Keno and the Gold Room at the Bank followed.

August 11: "Early in the morning, I took the bus for Whitehorse. We had a good view of the Five Fingers on the Yukon as well as a good view of Lake Le Barge. I changed buses at Whitehorse and set off for Edmonton. When midnight came, I was still on the bus."

August 12: "Going out I saw the sunset in the Rockies and now returning I saw sunrise in the Rockies. This time I had a good view of Muncho Lake - It is very long and beautiful. Twelve kilometers of jade-colored water will tell you that you have reached Muncho Lake. You have the choice of camping at Strawberry Flats campground or at MacDonald campground, 11 km further north. The lake's cold, deep waters, tinted green by minerals, are home to lake trout, arctic grayling, bull trout and whitefish.

I also had a good view of the Liard River and saw some deer early in the morning. We spent the night at Dawson Creek."

August 13: "We left at 7:30, crossed over the Smoky River, the Liard, the Peace, and also the Athabasca arriving in Edmonton about 5 p.m."

August 14: "After a good night at the King Edward hotel, I left at 7:30 a.m., passed Vermillion, only 80 miles from Louise. On to Saskatchewan and North Battleford, a very active town and to Saskatoon where I had a good view of the University. Then the open prairies with sloughs full of ducks."

Soon they were in Manitoba and arrived in Winnipeg. An hour later, they were into Ontario. Next, that long drive through miles of scrappy spruce. By evening they had arrived at Port Arthur which is now amalgamated into Thunder Bay.

"The bus was crowded, so I had to share my seat which made for a poor night."

August 16: "At 6:25 in the morning, we arrived in Sault Ste. Marie and I took a taxi to Aunt Sadie's. I had breakfast and went to bed. Marion came for dinner in the evening."

The next day she took the bus to the farm. While there, she visited with some very good friends, including a delightful afternoon and evening with Muriel McPhee who had visited her in Nassau.

"Muriel drove me to Chub Lake and after dinner showed her pictures of South America, which were very good."

As happens several times in her journals, pages are missing so we miss her trip back to Nassau.

Her conclusions: "My summer in Canada, mostly with relatives, was only partially a success."

She had had an unfortunate misunderstanding with my parents, which left her feeling that the fellowship and kinship had been broken. "I can never again look on the farm as a home. I would always wonder if I am really welcome."

As with all of us, her attempts to 'read' people were not always trustworthy. In that insecurity that we have noted several times, she misread my parents completely, which no doubt coloured her thinking about the entire trip.

Back in Nassau once more she says, on October 11, 70, "My summer is over and I am back at school. I have given up the Red Cross."

We don't have much information about GHS during this fall term, but at mid-term break, October 31, she and a teacher friend had a lovely six-hour sail to the Island of Eleuthra where they stayed at the Hatchet Bay Club but they were not made to feel very welcome. Most of the tourist places were shut down.

The next day, they rented a car and drove around South Eleuthra. On November 2, they drove over the north of the island. On November 3, they caught the boat for home. In spite of the difficulties, she describes it as a glorious trip.

November 4: "I spoke to the Ladies Bible Class at Trinity. 'The weeds in the wheat.' Matthew 13: 24 – 30. There were just 7 ladies present but it was very enjoyable."

This was a fairly frequent occurrence and shows that in spite of her seeming religious ambivalence, she still retained a love of teaching the Bible when given the opportunity. No, she has not lost her faith, even if we might question some of the changes in her lifestyle.

Always an astute observer, Reba reports in the fall of 1970, "There is a great uproar going on in our black government. Four leading men have broken away and are trying to unseat Pindling and put Wallace-Whitfield in instead. It is said by these dissidents that before Christmas there will be a very real economic crisis here."

This suggestion of rebellion in the PLP was not just in Reba's imagination. Writing in *Islanders in the Stream*, Craton and Saunders state: "Far more damaging to the PLP were the defections toward the right, which gradually led to the reorganization of parliamentary opposition. The process began at the party convention in October 1970, when Cecil Wallace-Whitfield[60] attacked 'creeping totalitarianism' and resigned from his ministerial post. A few weeks later, Randol Fawkes introduced a non-confidence motion and eight PLP members voted with the UBP. They came to terms with the UBP members and formed a new party called the Free National Movement (FNM), which became the official opposition early in 1972."

December 18: "School closed today for the Christmas holiday with a carol service which was not much appreciated."

And so, 1970 came to an end as she headed into 1971 and more complications.

---

60   Craton and Saunders, *Islanders in the Stream*, p. 357.

Chapter Fourteen

More Complications

"Nothing worthwhile is ever without complications."

— Nora Roberts

"Nassau is an interesting place these days," Reba wrote in early 1971. "Pindling is crushing every scrap of opposition to himself. He is taking more and more into his own hands.

"Pindling has great power. Something is terrorizing those who would stand against him – is it communism, or the mafia?" asked Reba. "The government is hounding out everyone who dares to oppose. The secretary of the PLP resigned and fled to Freeport. Now the treasurer has resigned. Pindling is shaping up as a dictator."

In fact, the dissension had begun earlier. As we saw in the last chapter, in October, 1970, Cecil Wallace-Whitfield led a revolt at the PLP Convention, attacking "creeping totalitarianism". A motion of non-confidence was introduced by Randol Fawkes, and eight members of the PLP formed a new party called the Free National Movement (FNM).

Although Reba's suspicions were never confirmed, Craton and Saunders do suggest that the Mafia[61] were involved in gaining casino licenses for Grand Bahama, Freeport-Lucaya, and Paradise Island. A *Wall Street Journal* article in 1966 claimed that princely 'consulting fees', i.e. bribes, were paid to leading figures in the UBP leading to the PLP victory in the 1967 election. Reba expresses her fears that one of these powers was now working behind the scenes in the PLP.

---

61   Craton and Saunders, *Islanders in the Stream,* p. 343, 344.

At this time, the Bahamas Police Force was expanded to become the Bahamas Defense Force by the purchase of four fast-armed motor vessels with their crew trained by officers of the Royal Navy.

Reba was concerned about these changes. Can this be the man whom she had met shortly after arriving, and whom she described as "A soft-spoken and cultured man"? Is this "the cultured black Bahamian, a speaker for the Progressive Liberal Party (PLP) which champions the rights of the coloured people and the underdog?"

Now, it is different. "Self is on the throne. The one standard of life is to make money and get social position. Principle, right and decency simply don't exist. There is no one who can stand up for justice or righteousness."

Reba wrote: "It is so clear when people turn their backs on God, He turns His back on them. Man is not supreme. God is supreme. He has left the people here to the power of Satan. The people have been lulled to sleep and they can't do a thing."

Into these troubling circumstances came cousin Geoff from Ottawa.

"Last evening, I had just gotten my dinner over and had my things all ready for a quiet evening of studying Spanish and a time in prayer when the phone rang and I heard, 'Geoff, here.'"

This appears to have been a surprise visit. As we have seen, Geoff was no longer her favourite person. He continuously corrected her, which she did not like. When she showed him the four new police boats, he immediately lectured her on how the Bahamian Government would use these boats. These were just for protection of the harbour.

In fact, Reba was quite right: Craton and Saunders report that, "The tiny marine division of the Bahamas Police Force formed in 1971 was greatly enlarged. Trained by officers seconded from the Royal Navy, and initially provided with four fast armed motor vessels, the Bahamas Defense Force was soon engaged in warning off and rounding up poachers, smugglers and illegal immigrants."

Geoff's attitude annoyed Reba. She saw him to be like his mother who decides things she knows nothing about.

"Last summer, he embarrassed me greatly by saying no old maid was going to get him, for statistics proved that when a man lives as a bachelor as long as he has, they never marry."

March 24, 1971: "Geoff has gone. If he had stayed much longer, I'd have let him have it. He is not an attractive person. He has always been very self-centred. He has no religion whatever. In fact, I believe he has a very real resentment toward religion."

Although Reba so often appears to be conflicted about religion, denominations, and church, and although she appears to have adopted a rather worldly lifestyle since coming to the Bahamas, here is ongoing evidence of the fact that she has never lost her faith or confidence in God.

Reba had other concerns during this year as well. In January, her elderly friend Oliver Hunter, whom she had helped so much, called and asked her to come to see him. He had formed a company to manage his money and appointed Reba as one of two directors. It is called the Sunnor Company. A man named Cecil Cartwright was the other director. She signed the papers needed. She says, "Oliver seems very pleased with himself."

"Oliver is a rich man, just a bit more than a millionaire. His god is mammon (money) and all else takes second place. Even his loved sister Margaret was sacrificed on the altar of mammon. With all his money, Oliver keeps living in this outrageous fashion, moving from one hotel or rooming house to another, always thinking that someone is stealing from him. He moved to the home of a coloured lady, Pearl Cox. No doubt he got a cheap rate but he soon learned that there was very poor water pressure and a very frowsy kitchen. He found the place impossible, so on July 7, he moved to the Royal Elizabeth Hotel. It was better. The people at the desk were very kind and he seemed settled. Of course, it was only a hotel room. The air conditioner was no good so the room was very hot. The pool was empty and the garden was overgrown with weeds with no attempt to keep it up. But the room was clean and decent.

"He has sacrificed everything - comfort, family, even his beloved sister and his health as well. His money comes first - all else must be sacrificed and put second. What utter folly!

"Yet I accept him on his own terms.

"Oliver showed yesterday that he doesn't fully trust Cecil Cartwright. Cecil is always saying that Oliver must prepare for his death by taking someone into his confidence. Now Cecil is saying that Oliver can't live alone. Cecil keeps saying somebody must know what to do if anything happens.

"I can see now what he wants. He wants Oliver to be incapable and so he will be made executor of the estate. Oliver is fully aware of this, even though his eyesight is deteriorating fast.

"The old man is ill and in a nasty position for he has the good will of no one. He is a very ill man needing medical attention. But I fear he has made himself obnoxious to Dr. Rodgers and, as a result, he has very little interest in the old man. No one but myself cares about him."

There had been change at the school. Al David had been let go, which didn't surprise her. "They still intend to get rid of the expatriates. The ministry also sent a team to GHS today to find out why the results had been so bad. The whole discussion centred on the weakness of the students, not on any failure on the part of the teachers."

With spring break, Reba and her friend Margaret flew to North Andros. The plane had a capacity of 19 people. "At the airport on Andros, we contacted the driver for the Andros Beach Hotel, a nine-mile drive through the pine forests. We were assigned to Villa 33, about 1/4 mile from the hotel - a delightful little cottage with a good living room, a kitchen, bathroom and a bedroom for each of us. We went to the 4:30 Happy Hour at the Hotel for free drinks and cold conch fritters. We had dinner at the hotel, and walked back through the lovely night."

The next day they hired a mini-bus for the day and set off to see as much of the island as possible. They saw a number of places including one from which we could see the new bridge. They drove across the bridge to a hotel called the Stafford Arms. They visited Stafford Creek, a good-sized town out on an island reached by a causeway. "Many of the houses are built on stilts.

There are many palm trees which gives the place a distinctive look."

They travelled on through more communities to the Lighthouse Club, the largest hotel on Andros, a really seedy looking establishment. The road was wide and terribly dusty so they got very dirty as the minivan was all open. "As we had the car for 24 hours, we went for a drive through Nicoll's Town to Conch Sound, a rather small place. All these places are on the shore since Andros until recently had only water transportation connections. Some fairly decent houses and a lot of shacks. In the afternoon, as we lay on chairs on the beach, a fishing boat came in and they had caught a big blue marlin. We found the people of Nicoll's Town sweet and friendly, generally ignorant but gentle and loveable. We went to the Happy Hour and had a Bahama Mama. Then went back to the villa and made an omelet. We had it with ice cream for dessert."

April 18, 1971: "After breakfast we went to the hotel to settle up - $106.50 for 3 days. We were driven to the airport."

At the school, Reba experienced another example of the cleavage between black and white. "This morning I had Dr. Doris Johnson at the school to speak to the 4th form on religion.

"She was very different from what I had expected. She seemed like a very humble woman. The first period was given to her address. Her religion is mainly psychological and extrasensory perception. But she gave a well-thought-out address even if I couldn't always agree. She said, 'Call it God, call it Mohammed, call it Buddha.'

"To me these intuitive experiences are the Holy Spirit and I could never mix them with anything such as obeah (a native religion).

"The second period was given over to questions. Afterwards, she and I had tea in the cookery room. She told me how she had been very poor as a child but her mother's religion and faith had always been like a rock in their midst, something giving meaning and strength to the family. But as we sat having tea, I was aware that across the table from me was a closed face. I was the white woman. Between she and I there was no bridge – no real contact."

May 17: "Today I had another example of that difference. I had hair done and rushed off to a Spanish Class. I have been much interested in my Spanish teacher, Dr. Davidson Hepburn. He is so charming and cultured on the surface. A Negro from Old Bight - Cat Island. But underneath I find exactly the same thing that I felt with Dr. Johnson. You just can't reach him. There has been such a deep cleavage between the black and the white here. The Negro no longer values the white man's friendship. There is a rising tide of blacks who want to make the Bahamas a black country. They no longer feel honoured to be with white people. The white Bahamian sees this very clearly but not the ex-pat who still hopes to make his home here and thinks he can do it."

June 25: "I should have gone to Speech Day but didn't. We had such a bore of a staff meeting.

"How some of these teachers do love the sound of their own voices. They go off the subject, don't finish what was started and discuss student after student who shouldn't be discussed at all."

As the school year once again wound down, Reba attended a party for those who were leaving the school and the country. At the same time, she was having her vaccinations for another trip, this time to Africa.

On July 26, 1971, she began her journey to Africa as a representative to the world conference of the YMCA and YWCA. She does not mention how she came to be appointed to represent this organization, nor who funded the journey.

On July 27, she arrived in Luxembourg, and took the train for Paris. After a few days of sightseeing in Paris, she went to the airport, where she met members of the Canadian group. They arrived in Ghana, by way of Rome, where the plane was held up because of the heat.

"We flew out over the Mediterranean, and then over the coast of Africa. Soon we were over the desert. Below us we could see the cone shaped piles of sand, waves of sand and flat patches."

Ghana:

"When we arrived at the airport in Accra, the capital of Ghana, we were met by the Ghana YWCA. It was 11 p.m. before we arrived at our destination where confusion reigned. Our accommodation at the University of Ghana was very poor.

"On August 4, I awakened to the sound of a bird with a beautiful song which I had never heard before. I stepped out on my small balcony and for the first time looked on Africa."

It was perfect timing since the best option, weather-wise, is to visit Ghana in July and August, since there tends to be less rain during this time in the north, and generally no rain in the south.

During the next few days, she was treated to a number of delightful Ghanaian meals, including one at the home of the Minister of Health - fufu and palm nut soup and cassava.

She experienced the first sessions of the YMCA and YWCA Council. After listening to a discussion on the joining of the YWCA and the YMCA she got involved in a discussion group where her ideas of Christianity were opposed by an African-American woman who was quite violent in her attitude. She then clashed with a black woman who calls herself a Canadian. She decided to not take further part in the discussions.

August 8: "This morning I went to the Methodist Church. The service was in English and Ghanaian."

Over coming days, she went to a reception given by the Minister of Culture at the State House, saw the President's house, as well as many squalid towns. With their group, she was received by the Ashanti king and had a party at the Residency given by the commissioner. She went to the palace of the permanent chief of the Ga where they were entertained at a public reception. She enjoyed a luncheon put on by the Ghanaian ladies in the State House, then back to Council meetings.

August 16: "Prime Minister Busia came to the Council. He brought his whole cabinet with him. He addressed the Council. In the afternoon I went in to Accra."

On August 17, she spent the day at Council, morning, afternoon and evening, but felt that little was accomplished. Many talk of how uninteresting the meetings are.

But then things changed. "Five of us set off on a Speedway Tour bus for Akosombo.

"To be away from the crowds and the racket was glorious. We drove to Tema (a city on the Atlantic coast of Ghana) and saw the port, then to the Volta Dam.[62] It is very beautiful. We had lunch at Abiri Botanical Gardens and went to a reception given by the World Council of the YWCA at the Accra 'Y'.

"On August 20 the World Council of the YWCA came to a close with a rehash of all."

---

62 The Akosombo Dam, also known as the Volta Dam, is a hydroelectric dam on the Volta River in southeastern Ghana in the Akosombo gorge and part of the Volta River Authority.

Ethiopia:

August 21 saw some of the group fly to Ethiopia, stopping in Khartoum, the capital, and largest city of Sudan and the state of Khartoum, located at the confluence of the White Nile, flowing north from Lake Victoria, and the Blue Nile, flowing west from Ethiopia.

"We arrived in Addis Ababa where we went off to an excellent lunch at the 'Y'. It rained, was cold and muddy."

On August 24, they left Addis and arrived in Nairobi[63] where they went on a tour of the Nairobi Game Park. At the Treetops, which were very rustic, she saw one elephant, many Cape buffalo, some deer, and seven rhinos.

Tanzania:

On August 29, she arose very early and was off to Zanzibar, a semi-autonomous region of Tanzania in East Africa. It is composed of the Zanzibar Archipelago in the Indian Ocean, 25-50 kilometres (16-31 mi) off the coast of the mainland, consisting of many small islands and two large ones: "The Arab influence is strong here."

Zambia:

August 30: "We left Dar es Salaam for Zambia and were taken to the Ridgeway Hotel, a good hotel. In the afternoon we had tea at a YMCA member's home, but I would have preferred to be out seeing the country. We saw the House of Parliament and in the evening went to a buffet dinner at the 'Y' and a party afterwards."

September 1: "We rose early, were taken to the airport and flew to Kitwe. Kitwe is the second largest city in terms of size and population in Zambia. It is one of the most developed commercial and industrial areas in the nation, alongside Ndola and Lusaka."

---

63 Nairobi is the capital and largest city of Kenya. The name comes from the Maasai phrase *Enkare Nairobi,* which translates to "cool water", a reference to the Nairobi River which flows through the city. The city proper has a population of 3,138,369, while the metropolitan area has a population of 6,547,547.

On September 2, they arose early and flew back to Lusaka, then to Livingstone where they had a tour of the glorious Victoria Falls and a very enjoyable sundowner cruise on the Zambesi River.

September 3: "At last, we were off to the airport and a Zambia Airways flight to London. From there, we flew into Nicosia, Cyprus. What a thrill it was to be in a place where once the apostle Paul travelled."

The next day they flew back to London, to Luxembourg, and took the long flight back to Nassau.

What a trip!

On September 7, Reba returned to school, once again wishing it were over. Anatol Rodgers had been appointed headmaster. Reba felt that Anatol was far too weak to cope with this responsibility.

But Reba's view was not shared by other teachers nor the Board of Education.

Obviously, Anatol was a very capable woman as evidenced by the fact that she was only the second Bahamian woman to be appointed head of a school.

A good teacher friend of Anatol, Arlene Nash, writes: "Anatol tutored her own children for two years or so. Her son, Jonathan, became an eye surgeon while her daughter, Dr. Patricia Rodgers, became a diplomat and High Commissioner to Canada and other high posts."

Arlene continues, "Anatol was so revered that she was able to tell the Ministry of Education what she wanted. Everything had to be completely right. She was a most intelligent and dignified human being."

The fact that Anatol was highly valued by the Ministry of Education is confirmed by the fact that in later years, a new high school was named after her.

In 2012, Prime Minister Hubert Ingraham opened The Anatol Rodgers High School in Nassau with high praise for Mrs. Rodgers. "It was shortly after the school opened its doors in September, 2008 that the Government agreed to rename it in honour of Anatol Rodgers. We believed that this outstanding educator was due to have this modern state-of-the art edifice named in her honour.

"We are here to honour and memorialize the work of a fine citizen-educator, who committed her life and her considerable talents to teaching, one of life's noblest vocations. She made her mark in the field of education through encouraging her students to do their best. She believed in Bahamians' ability to achieve, and hence she provided the environment where they could so. Many of our finest citizens emerged during her tenure as Principal of the Government High School.

"Anatol Rodgers was a Reeves, the daughter of Lucille Robinson Reeves and C.H. Reeves after whom a Junior High School is named – the C.H. Reeves Jr. High School. I believe that this is the first time in our history that a father and daughter share such a distinction.

"Anatol Rodgers was a woman of stellar character. At the core of her character was the ability to discern the good and the possibilities in the character of her students, including those of whom some others had long thrown up their hands in frustration. Mrs. Rodgers was a model of public service and active citizenship. She attained many firsts in the institutions to which she dedicated her considerable energy. Most notably she became the first female head of the legendary Government High School, an institution to which she dedicated much of her life."

I wish that my cousin could have appreciated fully the character and ability of her friend. As I wrote to Anatol's daughter Patricia, "It appears that her early experiences of teaching these youngsters in their blue and white uniforms were very positive, and she certainly considered your parents to be good friends. But as the years went on, she became disillusioned. Her change of attitude was not without reason. In fact, Dr. Saunders's book *Islanders in the Stream* bears out a lot of Reba's reactions as justified. They say, 'Expatriates began to feel more and more alienated and unwanted, even though they were needed.'[64]

"Perhaps part of it was a case of two strong-minded women. When your mother became head, my cousin may have found it difficult to be under another woman. That has been known to happen I believe."

October 6: "I gave my first address on my trip to Africa at the YWCA adult group. I spoke on Ghana: as a tourist sees it. There were 18 present."

October. 8 "Went to the I.O.D.E. (International Order of the Daughters of the Empire) tea in the afternoon. It was very pleasant meeting people."

October 20: "Speaking again, this time to the Ladies' Class - There were 10 ladies present and I spoke on Psalm 46 and my trip to Africa, including

---

64 Craton and Saunders, *Islanders in the Stream*, p. 353.

visiting Victoria Falls and the area of David Livingstone. It was a very pleasant meeting."

November 5: "I received a telegram from Aunt Mabel. Uncle Lew has passed away. He is to be buried on Saturday."

Yes, it was true. Far away, back in Canada, in Thessalon, Ontario, my dad had passed away. But what Reba could not know was that something wonderful had happened which took the sting out of Dad's death for my mother and myself. A little woman from the Thessalon Bible Chapel, whom my dad would not ordinarily pay attention to, had visited him in hospital. I am not entirely sure what she said to him, but through her, God spoke to my dad. He had been a faithful churchgoer all his life, but in response to her questions, Dad acknowledged that he had never really said, "Yes" to Jesus. That day he experienced a new relationship with the Lord which led him to say to me not long before he died, "You know that Mrs. McDougall? She preached a better sermon to me, in about 20 minutes than I ever heard from any preacher."

Reba could not have known from Mom's telegram that we believe that Dad did not just die on November 5th, but entered into the presence of the Lord. 'Absent from the body; present with the Lord.'

December 17: "Today we had a Christmas service and then off for the holiday. The students in the gallery were awful. They talked, made fun of the service and misbehaved. It was amazing afterward to hear the teachers whitewashing it all or giving trite solutions. There is a serious problem in the school. They resent the white teachers and feel free to show it."

As we have noted, Reba's disillusionment caused her to continually long to leave Nassau but once again, her desires were not satisfied as she entered 1972. But there was an upside. Her very frustration gave her a good reason to travel.

CHAPTER FIFTEEN

Death - and Life - 1972

"Death is not the greatest loss in life. The greatest loss is
what dies inside us while we live."

— Norman Cousins

Oliver Hunter, her rich friend, was dying, needing someone with him at all
times. Reba did her best, looking after his accounts, preparing meals, changing bedding and getting him to his appointments.

"I had dinner with Oliver tonight and helped him with his accounts. He
really needs me, as he can no longer figure things out by himself." This was a
constant occurrence.

But of course, there was much else going on in her life.

There was her relationship with Martin Pounder and his sister Jean who
were living in the next apartment. Though there was a time when she might
have considered marrying him, she now says she is seeing too much of the
Pounders. Jean had come from England to bring Martin home. She had the
idea that he should go into an old folks' home in England but he wanted
nothing to do with that idea. Reba often made meals for them and they did
a great deal together, yet she did not enjoy Jean's company. Though they took
a cruise together to Fort Lauderdale at spring break, Reba describes Jean as a
bitter, frustrated woman. When they left for England at the end of April, she
says, "I was sorry to see Martin go but not Jean."

There was school. Drugs had been discovered at the school and Reba had
seen the people involved, but when she reported it, she got into trouble. She
decided, never again.

On January 31, she wrote: "A very unpleasant day at school followed by a miserable Parent Teachers' Association meeting." On another occasion she was threatened by a student with a second confrontation the day following but nothing was done about it.

As part of her responsibilities, she attended a Convention of Teachers on gaining independence for the Bahamas. "The speaker from the government gave a nasty, embarrassing speech." At the whole convention, she felt that there were poor speeches with little planning or thought. "We were forced to attend. We are civil servants who can take no part in politics."

I am so glad that we have the testimonies of students and fellow teachers, which I reported earlier, because they help to give a much more positive outlook on this period of Reba's life.

There was her involvement with the YWCA. "In the evening, I had a nominating committee meeting for the 'Y'.

"On April 15, we had our YWCA annual luncheon. A lovely lunch, a good program in a lovely setting. A most enjoyable affair. There were 130 present."

There was her steady round of social activities: dinner parties put on by others and by herself; golf, shows, all part of her usual busy life.

And there was her concern for the Bahamas. "The Bahamas continue to go down. The Lighthouse Club at Fresh Creek is in liquidation. Many hotels are almost empty. Six thousand homes are for sale on this island."

Craton and Saunders [65]confirmed: "Though Freeport-Lucaya was the area most obviously affected, the early 1970's was a period of economic and political crisis for the Bahamas as a whole.

"The Bahamas Christian Council argued that despite government's auditing attempts and regulations, no Bahamian should play the casinos, nor work for them. The casinos are inherently demoralizing, offering illusory promises of unearned wealth and temptations of corruption that far outweighed the benefits of ancillary employment or increased government revenue".

As an aside from her biographer, I would interject my endorsement of this comment. Unfortunately, in Canada the governments themselves have become addicted to the money from gambling.

---

65   Craton and Saunders, *Islanders in the Stream,* p. 356 see note re: gambling.

May 2: "Today we learned that Lew Morgan, former headmaster, has been told that he need not come in to the ministry of Education, nor come back. He was a poor, weak, and inefficient person but still it seems cruel."

As I read about these things, my mind goes back to her early days at the school when, having resigned from ministry and having spent five years in a convent, she was ready to face a new challenge. As there were trials in her ministry years, so there were challenges in teaching Religious Knowledge and English to the students of Government High School. We have struggled along with her in the joys and sorrows of those various encounters.

All of this was taking place while she watched over her elderly friend.

She had the feeling that the manager of the Trust Company was trying to get control of Oliver's estate. The manager was unhappy with Reba's presence in their meetings with Oliver as they did not want the old man to train her to carry on in his place.

Some would claim she was looking after him because she was a gold digger, seeking her own benefit. This would be both unkind and untrue. I find in the concern and compassion which she showed toward the old man a continuing response to the words of Jesus, 'Assuredly, I say to you, inasmuch as you did it to one of the least of these, my brethren, you did it to Me.' She could never really get away from her true motivation for ministry. Like many of us, she might change jobs but her basic love for God and for others did not change.

May 13: "I made supper for Oliver. His friend Cecil Carter, the other trustee of Oliver's Sunnor Company, came to talk about plans if Oliver should suddenly die. Oliver flew into a dreadful rage. The old man is terrified of death and the thought of leaving his precious money. He is failing fast and every time I go, I see further evidence of his going blind."

On May 28, Reba went to church, then made dinner for him. "He is now blind and is suffering still further weakness."

At 8:30 in the morning, June 4, "Mrs. Roberts called to say she could not rouse him. I went over and we called the doctor who put him in the hospital. I went to tell Eric Blanchard at the Trust Company. Later, I visited the hospital. Oliver seemed more himself and tried to talk but I could not make out what he was trying to say.

"In the morning I went to see him in hospital. He seems to have rallied a bit.

"I went to Trust Corporation where I met Mr. Caldwell, Mr. Peter Johnstone and Eric. Eric and I went to lawyers where papers were handed in that I had signed on Friday. The Trust Corp. has sweeping Power of Attorney on the estate."

On June 6: "Oliver knows me, but that is all I can say. He has refused to eat. He is steadily going down. He turns his head when I call his name but that is all."

"After school on the 9th, I went to Lawyer Hatchard's office with the seal and register for Sunnor Incorporated. In the evening I went to the hospital where I met Cecil Carter and we had a directors' meeting."

I can't help but wonder what this directors' meeting could accomplish, since all is now in the hands of the Trust Company, and Reba and Cecil had no say even in planning a funeral.

On the 14th, she went again to the hospital. Oliver continued to go down. On Sunday, June 18, she was again with him for over an hour in the evening before going home. At 9:30, Cecil called to say he was gone. "So, the long, weary, self-centred life is over." Reba had never backed off from her loving care for this old man. I am sure that she felt the loss. As in the case of an alcoholic whom my wife and I took into our home for several months, there is a sadness to see a life given over to an inadequate goal.

In assessing his life, I wonder if Reba still remembered and believed Hebrews 9:27: "It is appointed for men to die once, but after this the judgment."

On Monday, she met with four of the Trust Company officers and presented the key to Oliver's safety deposit box. "It was most interesting to see those men descend on that vault. There were two wills, one contradicting the other and going around in circles. Meanwhile, Lawyer Hatchard claimed that he had Oliver's will in his office. Strange dealings.

"On Tuesday at 6 p.m. old Oliver was laid to rest in Ebenezer Cemetery. Only prayers were recited. There were just eleven people present plus the minister. The lawyer was not told about the service though he wanted to attend."

Throughout this whole experience, Reba had reason to wonder about the honesty of the Trust Company who were serving as executors. They claimed that they had notified the heirs regarding Oliver's estate. Eric told her that there was a doctor in Vancouver who has four children who were the heirs.

"They claim that the Trust Corp is in touch with this man. But if he knows the estate is worth $1,700,000, why has he not rushed to Nassau to protect his children's rights? There were no answers available."

Personally, I find it amazing that with all the time my cousin was with this man, and all of the work she did on his accounts, she had never heard from him about family members or heirs to his estate. Could it be that as in the case of so many, he could not bring himself to think of the possibility that he was going to have to leave all of this behind?

"Eric seems to suggest that I will get nothing out of this estate at all. This really doesn't bother me, as God is far beyond Eric Blanchard or even Oliver's money."

So, Oliver is dead. But Reba was still very much alive!

June 29: "Last day of school - a very boring staff meeting. I applied to become a guidance counsellor, but it looks as if I am not to get this. These are days of farewells as one person after another leaves this colony."

July 2, 1972: "At church I had a beautiful feeling of the nearness of God. It was all my own and in no way connected to the service."

As we have tracked with her through these years, how thankful we can be that all of these experiences were relieved by her periodic travels – to Jamaica in 1957; to ten countries of Europe in 1968; to all four countries of Great Britain in 1969 and to Texas and Louisiana in 1970. Now she is planning a trip to Israel.

As I said in the foreword, Reba kept such careful notes about everything, that to read her journals is to be there with her, seeing what she saw and experiencing life as she experienced it. Several things are constantly in view: the quality of hotels she stayed in, the quality of the food, and the cost of everything. When considering what to leave out, her insightful records make it difficult to shorten the story of her trip to Israel as much as might be desirable.

How I wish that everyone could read her fascinating descriptions. Of course, in these days, many people have had the opportunity to visit the far-flung regions of the world and you have your own scrapbooks of memories.

"Now, it is time to be off again," she wrote. "Thank the Lord for the experience of travel as a respite from the strain of daily living. So, Israel!"

World Traveller, Israel

August, 1972, Israel

Many people dream of a trip to the Holy Land and some have the opportunity to achieve their desire. One of my pastor friends has led tours of Israel many times.

For those who have a basic knowledge of the Bible, her journey will touch on many places with which you are familiar. On the other hand, many of my readers will not be as conversant with the places mentioned. I know that reports of a person's world wanderings rank right up there with sitting in a darkened room, watching a poorly done travelogue, so I will try not to bore my readers with following her footsteps completely but I hope that, as she visits this ancient land, you may find some things to be of interest.

July 30, 1972: "I boarded a plane for London where I met my friend and fellow teacher Margaret Thomas. Soon we were on a plane bound for Tel Aviv. We met Rev. Johnson and his wife, our tour guide, and the rest of the party who are also on the Inter-Church Travel Tour, 28 in all.

"As darkness came on, we could see the lights of Tel Aviv. I confess that as we prepared to leave the aircraft, I felt a certain tension.

"Late in the evening, our bus rolled into the famous city of Jerusalem and past the Damascus Gate of the Old City to our hotel. Our hotel is called 'The Holy Land', a cheap Arab hotel. Our room was comfortable, having a small balcony and private bath. The evening was pleasant with a cool breeze blowing through the room."

August 9: "We wakened in the city of Jerusalem. Sunrise comes early - around 4:30. We had our first breakfast - hard bread, supposed to be toast, coffee and a poor kind of marmalade, also, synthetic juice. A poor meal.

"We set off on a walking tour of the Old City. We entered by the Damascus Gate, walking into a world of narrow streets, of high buildings, so high that I got the feeling the streets were all covered. Small shops lined the streets. One didn't dare look around much for the streets are all on inclines and have very wide, shallow steps.

"All sorts of merchandise was before us - a butcher shop with the carcasses of sheep hanging in its front, a shop of trinkets and great trays of sticky looking sweets. They were dirty and smelly. Cars couldn't move on these streets, the only thing that could navigate them was a donkey and we met a good many of them. It was the typical Arab bazaar.

"Every now and again we would see a doorway and a narrow lane leading to the dwellings in these tall stone houses all so close together."

They were taken to the Church of Christ, where they had a commissioning service. Their guide was Gabriel Malta of Bethlehem who now guided them to a church which was said to be built on the place which was the home of Mary the mother of John Mark. It was supposed to be the upper room where Jesus instituted the Lord's Supper.

Next, they were taken through the narrow winding streets of Old Jerusalem to what was claimed to be the Holy Sepulcher.

Reba was not impressed by the validity of this site. Later we shall report on Gordon's Calvary as a much more likely Calvary and garden tomb.

"We closed our morning tour at the Roman pavement of the Praetorium of Pilate. It was the actual pavement on which Jesus had stood."

In the afternoon a bus drove them up to Bethany[66] where Mary and Martha and Lazarus lived. They visited the tomb of Lazarus whom Jesus raised from the dead. Outside it was interesting to stand and look up to the hillside, knowing that Jesus had definitely walked here and Mary and Martha had lived somewhere in this area.

"I never realized how much uphill it was for Jesus when he walked from Bethany to Bethphage and then into Jerusalem. The road was narrow with a deep gorge beside it, quite thrilling. Every sacred spot is covered by a church and at Bethphage there was one with a fine mural of the triumphant entry of Jesus."

On the Mount of Olives, they saw the church of the Pater Noster which had the Lord's prayer in 64 different languages, a big panel for each one. They then walked down a very steep path to the Garden of Gethsemane. They walked about the garden, which was lovely as so often pictured.

"As Margaret and I were very tired we made our way to the bus. We had a good chat with the Israeli driver, a second-generation Israeli. All the young men serve one month of every year in the army.

"We returned to the hotel finally at 6:15, had supper and went to bed after a terrific day, our bones fairly creaking from so much unaccustomed effort."

In the days that followed, they visited Jericho and caught a glimpse of the Dead Sea.

"It was very thrilling driving out into the wilderness of Judea. The great hills are all dry and brown at this time of year. We had our first sight of Bedouin encampments with their long low flat black tents. We saw shepherds leading their flocks of black goats and grey sheep. There is a lot of what looks like bunch grass and tumbleweed. We caught glimpses here and there of the old Roman road on which Jesus had actually walked.

"The City of Jericho is green with many date palms and fig trees. It is a complete contrast to the dry wilderness."

---

66 John 11:1 - 44

They visited Qumran[67] where they saw the mouth of Cave 4, in the mountain side. This was one of the caves where the Dead Sea scrolls had been found.

The Dead Sea scrolls found in this series of caves became world-famous, as they were copies of the actual Old Testament scriptures, transcribed about 200 B.C. The 800-plus manuscripts - written on papyrus or animal skin, stored in large clay pots with lids were discovered in caves by the Dead Sea in the late 1940s and 1950s, less than 20 years before Reba's visit to the area. They include virtually the only known Biblical documents written before the second century A.D. Almost every book of the Old Testament was included.

Comparing these earliest copies with the much later hand copied scriptures has revealed to Biblical scholars just how extremely accurate are the texts which we read as the Word of God. While they were in the area, the group set off for the Dead Sea for a swim. Changing in a rather rough place for dressing, they walked to the sea.

She says, "The stones were very hot and uncomfortable. The water near the shore was like a hot bath. We had about an hour here and then drove back to Jerusalem. It was a glorious morning and most enjoyable."

In the afternoon they went to Bethlehem. They passed by the Shepherd's Field where they were taken to a natural cave where the shepherds and their flocks used to shelter. Over this had been built a very beautiful church. It had three lovely murals of the shepherds. The first showed fear as the angel comes; in the second the fear is turned to adoration, and the third depicts great joy. In each was a dog which reflected clearly his master's feelings. The whole roof was made up of small windows so that the light came in from the ceiling.

They visited the church of the nativity, marked by two churches here, the Greek Orthodox and the Roman Catholic. They next saw a probable site of the birth of John the Baptist. "It was a lovely light church with round pictures around the dome and lovely tiles on the wall presented by Spain. There was a grotto. There were some lovely pictures (murals) of Mary meeting Elizabeth to tell her wonderful news.

"We set off for the museum which holds the Dead Sea Scrolls. The museum is very famous and we saw the scrolls, but the central one was not there. This is the complete manuscript of Isaiah. It is the oldest scripture manuscript in the world.

---

67   https://www.deadseascrolls.org.il/home

A photostatic copy is on display. In all essential points it is the same as our Isaiah translations. I felt a real thrill to think of how very precious it is. It really builds up one's faith to see these things. This scroll is beyond price."

August 12: Still in the area, they viewed the Kidron Valley, and the entrance to Hezekiah's water tunnel. "It was lovely clear water. It comes out at the Pool of Siloam."

They walked to the temple area and the mosque of Omar, "a beautiful building of bright blue mosaic work and lovely stained-glass windows. We took our shoes off outside and entered. The floor is covered with many Persian rugs. In the centre is the rock on which Abraham was about to slay his son Isaac and the angel intervened."

Their guide, Gabriel, told them that this rock was the real threshing floor of Araunah which David bought and later where the temple was built.

"We then crossed the temple area where we looked down at the wailing wall. We were away up high so we could see but in no way interfere with the activities at the wall. The wall has been beautifully cleaned and the whole place was very neat and clean. There were reading desks with red covers. The wall seemed to be divided: 3/4 for men and 1/4 for women.

"Next, we came to a site that is authentic, the pool of Bethesda.[68] We saw the small part of this that has been excavated. There is no water in it but the arches can be clearly seen and the actual steps down which friends had carried the lame man when he went to sit by the pool waiting for the waters to be troubled by an angel and where Jesus found him and healed him. We stumbled back through the Old City and out through the Damascus Gate to the hotel. We had had eight hours of solid sightseeing."

A big day followed. Down past Jericho and past Qumran, they headed southward along the Dead Sea. At places along this barren land around the sea, fresh water gushed out of the ground creating lovely green patches with juniper trees.

"The sea, sparkled in the sun and was quite attractive. We were travelling on a road which has only recently been completed and runs all the way right beside the Sea. In places there are sulphur and mineral baths, and there was also a small parchment factory.

"We came to a place where we turned off for Engedi or En Geddy as it is spelled here. There was one of these green patches here that was evidence of

---

68   John 5: 1 - 15

water. There was a long row of date palms near the road, places selling cold drinks beside which there was a path leading up. We did a very steep climb up very uneven rock steps, and through tunnels of vegetation, knowing there was running water nearby. Soon we saw the water and came to a delightful pool. On we went upward beside the stream until we came to another larger pool. It was intensely beautiful with great high rock walls on three sides. Over the top of one poured a slim, but lovely waterfall coming right down some 60 or 70 feet into the basin. This is a favourite bathing place for Israelis and there were a good many in the water. To this place came David and his companions when they fled from Saul. We should really have had longer to spend here. It is a historic monument kept by the Israeli government. We sat on the rocks for a while and rested before we started the steep downward climb. It is really something to be seen the way the water gushes out of these barren rocks. It is a never to be forgotten place. We made the long descent, had a cold drink and started off again.

"As we drove along, there was more evidence of salt. The shore of the sea was now rimmed with it as it is not in the north where the Jordan flows in. We saw what they call the tongue where the land comes out in a wide peninsula and the sea is very narrow. This tongue is in the country of Jordan so we were very close to the border. We were not able to see Jordan because it is on the border and we were not allowed to go there."

Just opposite to this on the Israeli side, rises the vast flat-topped rock of Masada.[69] Masada is famous as the fortress where the Jews made their last, desperate stand against the Romans.

The remains of the fortress can be reached by cable car.

"I wasn't the slightest bit nervous as it swung out into space and headed for the great rock. We watched the snaky serpentine path up the side of the rock. There was one hiker on it. It looked so very hot and we were thankful for the cable car. The sun blazed down and there was no shade at all. Getting

---

69 Masada—for many, the name evokes the image of a cliff rising dramatically above an austere desert landscape. The name is famously associated with the Masada siege, the final stand between the Jewish rebels and the relentless Roman army at the end of the First Jewish Revolt in 73/74 C.E. Trapped in the desert fortress-palace Herod built in the previous century, the rebels chose—as Jewish historian Josephus tells us—to commit mass suicide rather than be captured and enslaved by the Romans. Biblical Archeology Society

off the cable car, there were two steep, long flights of stairs to go up still farther before we were actually at the top.

"We saw where the Romans had built their great mound so that they could get level with Masada to attack. There was a fantastic view all about. We climbed up to Herod's upper palace and saw parts of a genuine mosaic floor that had been one of the rooms of his palace. This was wonderful to see but, oh! what a climb down in the blazing sun.

"Desperately tired, I went back to the cable car, and we all returned to our bus where we were each given a packed lunch. Of course, Engedi and Masada should not be taken together all in one morning. But this is a very cheap tour so we couldn't do otherwise."

Before returning to Jerusalem, they passed through the wild Judean country. They saw many Bedouin encampments, and came to the great Bedouin city of Beersheba but she says, all is changed. It is now becoming a modern place of industry. The Jews are living here and they do not look with favour on the Bedouins. This is the City of Abraham, but he was no Arab, though he was a Bedouin.

Another southern city was Hebron – an Arab place with flat topped houses of the same colour as the soil. They passed through the Valley of Eshcol[70] where the spies sent out by Joshua returned with abundant produce, but ten of them discouraged Israel from entering the land. She reports that the area was lovely, well-terraced and very fertile. Back to Jerusalem.

August 15, 1972: "We visited the Garden Tomb and Gordon's Calvary. The place of the skull was quite impressive. We saw the features of the skull quite clearly. The tomb captivated my attention. Stepping in, we saw clearly the place where Jesus' body lay and the place where the angel sat. I liked this place so much better than the Holy Sepulcher. The garden was quiet and there was no commercialism."

Travelling north, they had lunch at old Samaria.

"The highlight of our day came when we broke over a hill and got our first glimpse of Galilee. We got out of the bus to have a look and take pictures. We

---

70 Numbers 13:24 That place was called the valley of Eshcol, because of the cluster which the children of Israel cut down from there. Numbers 32:9 For when they went up to the valley of Eshcol, and saw the land, they discouraged the heart of the children of Israel, that they should not go into the land which Yahweh had given to them.

were then driven down to the Jordan River where it flows out of the Sea of Galilee. This was our first and only look at the Jordan River."

At Tiberius, on the west side of the lake, they were disappointed because their hotel was away up in the town, nowhere near the lake. They learned that no guide had been assigned to them. They had noticed throughout that Mr. Johnson was strongly biased in favour of the Arabs and didn't get on well with the Israelis. The next day, August 16: "Mr. Johnson was now both guide and leader and our driver knows no English, only Hebrew. Just one of Mr. Johnson's inadequacies as a guide."

From Tiberius, they continued north along the lake to the Mount of the Beatitudes, a small hill not far from Capernaum where Jesus preached his longest and best-known sermon. They stopped at a little rock bay, where Peter may have said 'I go a fishing.' Another horseshoe shaped bay would make a natural Amphitheatre where Jesus may have taught the multitudes from the water.

Capernaum, which became Jesus' home, was once a village of 1500 people. When Reba visited the area, there was no village and no homes. A famous ruin includes a synagogue, Roman columns and the supposed site of Peter's wife's mother's home.

"From Capernaum, we set off for Nazareth. We saw the new Nazareth up on a ridge but got no nearer. We were driven down to old Nazareth and to a restaurant run by a Mr. Nasar. Mr. Johnson was loud in his praise of this place. I wished we could have gone to Israeli Nazareth, but with Mr. Johnson that would have been quite out of the question. After lunch we were taken to a church built on the site, so we were told, where Jesus lived with his family. We saw just where the house was and the stable, then we all trooped down to a cave which was underneath. We were told all families had their caves under their houses to which they resorted in the hot weather."

The Church of the Annunciation was a very beautiful church built on three levels. It had a magnificent dome which is like the inverted petals of a lily, then on the top, a lighthouse or beacon.

From Nazareth, they went by launch across the lake to a kibbutz: Ein Gev. "The water was very calm so we had a pleasant trip. Since the Israelis were used to Christians wanting to pray in the middle of the lake, the boat stopped. It took about an hour to get across.

"We went to a part of the beach, and put down our things. We went inside the gate and saw the cottages where couples live and looked briefly into the dining hall. We went back to the beach and went bathing. The beach was very stony but the water was grand. We had a glorious swim. Then we got dressed and all went into an air-conditioned restaurant for a fish dinner. The fish are called Peter's perch. They served the whole fish on a small stainless-steel platter. It was sweet but very bony as perch always are. We finished rather quickly as the Jewish Sabbath was about to begin and the last boat back went at 1:30. The lake had gotten quite rough but as the ferry was a big strong boat, it just made the ride back more interesting."

August 19: "Margaret and I left by taxi for Hamat Gader[71] where we spent the day swimming and watching the view at Galilee. The water was delightful and we watched the changing light on the hills around Galilee. It was a lovely day. We were surrounded by Jews speaking a language we did not understand. These Jews of Israel are a real melting pot. Of course, none of the really religious ones were at the beach for this is their sabbath. We saw no skull caps and no side curls."

They were coming toward the end of their tour of Israel.

Reba's comment: "This is a very poorly planned tour. Far too much one day and not enough other days. Everything about the tour is cheap. The poorest buses on the road and the poorest hotels. I could not recommend Inter Church Travel."

August 20, 1972: "The special service was planned today for the YMCA in Migdal. They were taking communion. I went up and was surprised to see Margaret follow me. It is a lovely chapel. One end is all glass and looks right out over the lake. After the service, we all got cold drinks, and then went for a swim in the lake. There was a group of Arabs having a picnic there."

August 21: "Around 9:30 the bus came with a driver who knew not a word of English. We passed along the shore of Galilee and through Migdal, past the valley of the doves, with its many caves. The mountains here are almost 3,000 feet high. We went through a rather large town called Magyar. We saw a water channel which was most interesting. It is a real engineering feat carrying water from Galilee right down to some of the desolate little

---

71 Hamat Gader is a hot springs site in the Yarmouk River valley, used since the Classical antiquity. It is located in an area under Israeli control, in what was a demilitarized zone between Israel and Syria from 1949 to 1967. The site is next to the Jordanian border, and about 10 kilometres (6.2 mi) from the tripoint of Israel.

settlements. As a result, the level of Galilee has been lowered somewhat. This country is full of vast olive groves.

"We saw an ancient tell (hill) going back 2,000 years. We drove right to the old city with its vast crusader fortifications all along the Mediterranean. The sea broke on the rocks into white foam and there were jutting out old parts of broken walls. The vast fortifications are not all broken and many, many Arabs are living in them even when they are half tumbled down.

"Our driver now took us along the Bay of Haifa. The land was flat with many factories. The city of Haifa[72] climbs up the side of Mount Carmel. At one spot we all got out and had a look at the harbour below. We could see ships in the harbour and at the docks. We went on to a church supposed to be on the spot where Elijah looked to sea and saw the cloud arise, the size of a man's hand. Somewhere in this area, Elijah defeated the priests of Baal."[73]

From Haifa, they continued south to Caesarea. They saw the remains of an old aqueduct and the ruins of an Amphitheatre. This was the ruins of the Roman Arena in Caesarea, the place where Agrippa was smitten with worms because he made himself out to be God. "This is our last day in Israel. Tomorrow we are off to England."

August 22: "Our alarm went off at 10 to 4 in the morning. We went down to an early breakfast. These Israeli breakfasts are very queer. A buffet table is set up with large bowls of olives flavoured with garlic, cucumber slices, wedges of tomatoes, shelled, cold boiled eggs, cream cheese and jugs of yogurt. On the tables are hard rolls. Coffee and tea come around. Around 9, our plane flew off and we had an uneventful trip to London."

September 1, 1972: "I called Martin and said goodbye and the next day in the afternoon I left for Nassau on a Quantas flight."

September 4: "With great unwillingness I returned to school."

Back in Nassau, Reba was now watching the election which took place September 19, 1972. She took a strong interest in the results. There was a new party in these elections. When the eight members left the People's

---

72 Haifa is the third-largest city in the State of Israel after Jerusalem and Tel Aviv, with a population of 279,591 in 2016. The city of Haifa forms part of the Haifa metropolitan area, the second- or third-most populous metropolitan area in Israel. It is also home to the Bahá'í World Centre.

73 1 Kings 18: 19-40

Liberal party, they joined with those of the UBP to form 'The Free National Movement.' (FNM)

Doctors Craton and Saunders state, "Though there had not been a widespread demand for immediate independence, Pindling announced on June 14, 1971 that independence would be sought immediately after the next general election which was brought forward to September 19."

Craton and Saunders express the results in this way. "The general election… was an astounding victory for the PLP[74] and an unequivocal mandate for Bahamian independence. The FNM won only 9 seats to the PLP's twenty-nine. Every one of the eight former PLP candidates (who broke away) were defeated."

Reba says, "There will be a lot of upset people today. There have been so many fully self-centred people here who worship man and look on religion with a tolerant contempt. I know them in Government High School where they have crucified Religious Knowledge as a subject, making it a second-rate object of contempt. Ah, but God is still on His throne."

Perhaps, here we see one of the factors of her dissatisfaction with the school. She was obviously feeling that the main subject which she had been hired to teach was being downgraded in value, which would also downgrade her own position on the staff.

At the school, Reba continued to be disappointed.

October 5: "In the evening, we had a meeting with parents at the school. There were nine short speeches. The meeting was boring."

November 18,1972: "We had the YWCA Annual Thanksgiving luncheon held at the Flager Hotel. It was very good and an excellent crowd out."

December 19, 1972: "Today school broke up for the Christmas holiday. I left school as quickly as possible."

1972 had been a year which featured Oliver's death and her trip to Israel. Unfortunately, because of the poor quality of travel with Inter Church Tours, she found it disappointing.

But she was starting to look forward rather than backward, and the year ended with Martin Pounder coming back to Nassau to accompany her on a wonderful Caribbean Cruise.

---

74 Craton and Saunders, *Islanders in the Stream*, p. 358, 359.

Chapter Sixteen

Looking Forward, not Back

"Where I am at, is not actually where I am at. Where I am at is merely a point on the path to where I am going."

— Tony Cleaver

With another school term behind her, Reba once again looked forward to "getting away." With school closed for the Christmas holidays Martin Pounder was again in Nassau to accompany Reba on a cruise of the Caribbean.

December 25: Christmas at sea. "The company tried to make it festive. At dinner they put all the lights out and a small band came in to accompany a flaming Bobelu for dessert. It was a light cake with rum and meringue. Afterward we sang Christmas carols, but it did not go over well because many of the passengers are Jewish. It didn't seem like Christmas at all."

They enjoyed this time at sea. This cruise carried them past the coast of Cuba in the distance, to the Island of St Maartens,[75] and to Martinique.

"We came to St Pierre where once there was once a city of 44,000 people. All died when Mt. Pelee erupted and even the ships in the harbour were burned to the water line by the red-hot ash. Now only 5,000 people live in St. Pierre. They came to Barbados, and Trinidad, and Grenada. Every island is different."

---

75 St. Maarten, part of the Kingdom of the Netherlands, is a country on the southern part of a Caribbean Island shared with Saint Martin, a French overseas collectivity. Its natural features span lagoons, beaches and salt pans. The capital, Philipsburg, has cobblestone streets and colorful, colonial-style buildings lining its Front Street shopping area. The port is a popular cruise-ship stop.

On January 1, 1973, they arrived at the island of Antigua. On to San Juan, then St. Thomas-Charlotte Amalie.

Once again, in the distance they saw the coast of Cuba. On the 6th, the Sun Viking arrived in Miami, where they went through Customs and arrived back in Nassau.

She says of the holiday, "These cruise ships do present a delightful way of life. There is always plenty to do. I felt really sad saying goodbye to our really glorious ship."

January 7: "Today I went back to school. How dull after the glorious days on the Sun Viking!"

Her days at school continued to be heavy. Her other activities were demanding: a YWCA meeting at the headquarters; a YMCA luncheon; a Red Cross meeting entirely and successfully led by the girls; another YWCA meeting with little value.

I am sure that she also smarted over the awareness that some of her contemporaries looked on religion with a tolerant contempt. She said that "they had crucified Religious Knowledge as a subject, making it a second-rate object of contempt."

How that must have hurt. Already feeling unwanted as an expatriate, this suggests that she also felt that the school subject she had been hired to teach was not valued.

But while her contemporaries may have expressed contempt for religious knowledge, it remained important to her. There were many Bahamian kids who remembered her fondly even into their adult years.

She not only loved to teach high school students, she enjoyed teaching adults. "I went to the Ladies' Class and used my little lamp which I had purchased in Israel as the basis for my talk. I definitely felt that the Holy Spirit was really present with the group. It was a lovely meeting."

As many of us have experienced, her time away had given her time to reflect on the past months and years. We see a change of attitude as she began to look forward rather than backward. We hear less of her dissatisfaction with Nassau and the school and more of her plans for the future.

Martin helped her apply for a pension from the Department of Education. That was an important first step in thinking ahead to life beyond the Bahamas.

January 7: "I had an interesting letter from Eric Blanchet. I was told that I could put in a claim against the Hunter estate" (which she did).

Another step in that direction was applying for the position of assistant to the Minister in the Presbyterian Church in Victoria, B.C. Religion remained important to her and she was open to the idea of returning to ministry as she looked forward to returning to Canada.

Though they promised to consider her application, she did not get the position, but the action of applying helped her to look forward to the next step instead of looking back at past experience.

April 28: "Yesterday, I saw Mrs. Seymour at the Ministry of Education who gave me good hope of a pension. I spent the day writing up my application, which I will give to Anatol on Monday. Martin is a real help in these things."

May 30, 1973: "In the evening I drove Martin to the airport. I have enjoyed having Martin with me very much but as a man, he does have his limitations. You can never have a heart-to-heart talk to him. He doesn't want to listen to you or hear of any problems you may have. He wants to do the talking and get all the sympathy. In discussions, he has the answers and his mind is fixed. You could never influence him so you must just sit quiet and agree. He could never see himself in a fault."

I smile as I write this, because have we not heard this song before, not only about Martin but about Geoff, and about each of her roommates?

Although she was a strong, independent woman, perhaps even a woman ahead of her time, there were also insecurities which, like our own self-doubts, accompanied her throughout her life.

But Reba was not one to sit quiet and just agree. She had lived on her own for too long. She believed that it was a woman's right to speak and be independent. Being the second woman ordained in Canada, she had broken ground for women in ministry. She had lived and observed life in a new country. She had taken part in an international conference. She had travelled too far on her own without a man's help or approval.

No, she was not cowed by Martin Pounder or Geoff Miller, or by her brother-in-law, Wilbur Rogers, with their supposed superiority, knowledge and experience. But she did long for mutual respect, for heartfelt conversation and for the sharing of ideas. Many women share those desires.

At the same time, she did not wear her heart on her sleeve, and with her inscrutable nature, she could hold her peace and not let them know what she was really thinking about their pretensions.

Although she felt that she might miss Martin's company, she actually didn't. "I have enjoyed the day so very much, just doing as I like with no responsibilities at all. Really, I need this rest also."

We come now to something new in her journals. She begins to put in texts of scripture.

The first one is one of my favourites.

Psalm 37:3-6: "Trust in the LORD, and do good; Dwell in the land, and feed on His faithfulness. Delight yourself also in the LORD, and He shall give you the desires of your heart. Commit your way to the LORD, trust also in Him, and He shall bring it to pass. He shall bring forth your righteousness as the light, and your justice as the noonday."

Here is another indication that Reba has not forgotten dependence on the Word of God. Though her feelings have been altered by her exposure to a wide range of religious thought, and although she sometimes reacts against the "narrow" views which she once held and preached, it is good to see that she continues to read and profit from the scriptures.

Bahamian Independence:

Meanwhile, things were moving steadily toward independence for the Bahamas. The 1972 election, held on September 19, 1972 had been "an outstanding victory for the PLP. Above all it was an unequivocal mandate for Bahamian independence. For the first time, the opposition openly acknowledged that the Bahamas belonged to the black majority and attempted to fight the election on issues other than race."[76]

With that backing, the Progressive Liberal Party calmly but triumphantly led the Bahamas into independence.

In London, a multi-party Independence Conference worked through the details and the Bahamas Independence Bill passed its third reading in the

---

76 Craton and Saunders, *Islanders in the Stream,* p. 359, 360, 361.

British House of Commons by seventy-four to four and in the House of Lords by fifty to eleven, becoming law on June 12, 1973.

"The independence of the Bahama Islands, arguably the climactic achievement of the Bahamian people came into effect at midnight on Sunday July 9, 1973. The Union Jack was slowly lowered to the sound of the Last Post, and in its place, to the jaunty beat of the new national anthem, 'Lift up your heads to the Rising Sun, Bahamaland' the new national flag was hoisted proudly, the black triangle on stripes of aquamarine and gold said to represent the vigor and force of a united people determined to develop the rich resources of land and sea."

"Though matters of internal security, external defense, and foreign affairs had finally been handed over to the elected government, the Commonwealth of the Bahamas remained resolutely within the British Commonwealth with the Queen as head of state, represented by a governor general, who would henceforward be a Bahamian appointed on the advice of the ruling party.

"Sir Milo Butler [77] was appointed the first Governor-General of the Bahamas (the official representative of Queen Elizabeth II) shortly after independence."

Thus, as we have noted throughout this account, Reba was on hand for major turning points on numerous occasions during her lifetime.

Summer trip: 1973 - Canada

As soon as school was out, Reba set out on her next adventure. Travelling aboard the Flavia, she passed the Berry Islands and Bimini, arriving in Miami on July 2.

Leaving Miami by bus she travelled up through the centre of the state. An old man going to New York informed her that in New York, people lock themselves in their apartments, afraid of being attacked.

"What a condition the world is getting into!!!" she says, and we remember that this was 1973 - 45 years ago.

She arrived in Montreal, changed buses and went to Ottawa. "I finally reached Geoff at 10 p.m."

---

77   Craton and Saunders, *Islanders in the Stream,* p. 362.

She set off with Geoff in a circle through the upper states and back into Canada in order to visit past friends. This included time in Bramalea with her brother-in-law, Wilbur, where she met his new wife. She did not find this visit satisfying.

She says, "I haven't felt in the slightest bit at home here."

She went to Belleville where she had a good visit with her niece, Carol, and her husband, Bob, aboard Bob's 28-foot cabin cruiser before travelling by bus to Thessalon.

There, she again visited family and friends. She attended the Thessalon Bible Chapel and the gospel meeting at the Algoma Manor, and met Philip Norbo, the pastor. She found him to be an attractive young man but described his preaching as a narrow, conceited type of religion. "It is an interpretation of religion that appeals to so few people and rightly so."

This is an interesting comment since this solid biblical teaching was the content of her own early sermons. That she has not totally changed is revealed by including verses in her journal, and feeling the presence or lack of the Holy Spirit in various situations. She still retains a desire for a relationship with God, even though she no longer embraces her evangelical roots. This is all part of the challenge and change she experienced, first through her exposure to the liberalism of the United Church, then through her time in the Catholic Convent and her obvious inner conflict in what she considered to be the "cold" Methodist church in Nassau.

In this she is not unlike many others who remember their early Christian teaching, and rather wistfully long for it, while avoiding further exposure to the gospel. Thankfully, she was still reading God's Word and recording passages which touched her heart

On July 30, she began another trip to the west coast.

Thunder Bay, Winnipeg, across Manitoba and across Saskatchewan to Calgary. "Leaving Calgary, you break over a hill and there are the Rockies in front of you. What a thrill!

"Very soon we entered the Banff National Park. It is so very beautiful with the rivers and mountains. Then into Yoho with their wonderful glaciers which are quite inaccessible. It was a wonderful drive through Golden and Revelstoke also ringed by mountains. Then into the Okanagan Valley, and to Penticton."

In coming to Vancouver, she was meeting relatives on her mother's side whom she had met before but would now experience more fully.

Her cousin, Louise Douglas, was at the bus station to meet her.

August 6: "I had my first full day in Vancouver. It was quite something after 28 years to see all my cousins again.

"The Douglas' have a home at Boundary Bay, another one in Vancouver, and are building a third house in Richmond. Louise spends a lot of time looking at properties for sale."

After sharing in family dinners with the family and visiting Stanley Park, she went to Victoria. Louise Miller (Geoff's sister) met her at the bus station and they drove the 22 miles to Louise's home in Sooke.

"It is quite definitely a country place. There is a grand view from Louise's house and in clear weather the Olympic mountains of Washington can be seen. Louise's whole life is her home. She is putting everything she has into it."

August 12: "Today we went to Victoria to First United Church. I met the assistant pastor. We went to a coffee hour after the service held in honour of a 90-year-old minister.

"The next day, Louise drove me all around Victoria, including the Butchart Gardens. They were just lovely and I enjoyed seeing them very much. The roses and the tuberous begonias were especially lovely."

Up Vancouver Island they went, first on the scenic but dangerous Malahat Drive. She was looking forward to a good walk through Cathedral Grove near Nanaimo.

"It was really lovely, such great tall firs. We went as far as Port Alberni where we had dinner at the Tyee Village. Alberni is very beautiful all ringed with great mountains. On our return we went to Qualicum Bay and walked briefly on the beach. A lovely day."

August 15: "I returned to Vancouver. It was interesting passing the Gulf Islands and I could see the settlements on them. In Vancouver we had a final family picnic in Stanley Park. It was pleasant to think that perhaps soon Vancouver will be my home. I am looking forward to that day."

It was time once more to return to Nassau.

On August 16, she left for Portland, Oregon. She found Washington to be a rural and rather uninteresting state.

"I had a glorious trip along the Columbia River with several good views of Mount Hood and Mount Adams. On to Boise, Idaho, Salt Lake City and out into Wyoming. Had a good trip through Denver and Colorado.

"Near Colorado Springs the driver pointed out a mountain where there is an atomic base.[78] There is a veritable skyscraper in the mountain.

"Then we were rushing along through Texas. What a huge state! Houston - a good hotel and a good rest. Through Texas, into Mississippi, and into New Orleans. It was a rough night. I saw daylight around Tallahassee, Florida and finally arrived in Miami. I was worn out."

August 24: "In the morning I went to the Flavia cruise ship. I had a good dinner but went to my berth. I was too tired to do anything. The steward awakened me at 7:15. I rushed through breakfast, then off to immigration and off.

Home again in Nassau. As I was very tired, I had a complete rest today."

August 27: "Went to school today, As the students aren't there it was painless but we had been told that we had to be back by the 27th."

September 3: "A dull and unprofitable day at school."

She includes another bible text: "He that is mighty hath done to me great things and holy is his name." Luke 1:49

Another: 2 Thessalonians 3:3 "But the Lord is faithful, who shall establish you, and keep you from evil."

On Sunday, she again attended the Methodist Church at which she says the congregation was poor - not more than 100 people because so many have left the Bahamas.

She was still finding racial tensions. "At school, all whites are on shaky ground. The blacks don't want us around. They are going to get rid of us, perhaps sooner than we think."

By contrast, "I had a delightful time speaking to the Ladies' Class."

---

78 The Cheyenne Mountain Complex is located at Cheyenne Mountain Air Force Station (CMAFS), a short distance from NORAD and USNORTHCOM headquarters at Peterson Air Force Base in Colorado Springs, Colorado. Cheyenne Mountain Air Force Station falls under Air Force Space Command and hosts the activities of several tenant units. https://www.norad.mil/About-NORAD/Cheyenne-Mountain-Air-Force-Station/

October 19: "Today school was cancelled as there was a hurricane near the Bahamas. How lovely to have a day off school."

She reports on a meeting of Religious Knowledge teachers chaired by a former nun who came out of Orders. I am sure that she found this an interesting experience in light of her own time spent with the sisters in London, Ontario.

She had several of these.

On November 21, she says, "I had a very good meeting at the Religious Knowledge group, held at the Queen's College. We had a splendid discussion. A really good syllabus is being worked on."

November 27: "I went to St. Augustine's and talked to Sister Rita. They are so much better equipped than Government High School. It is so pleasant to be amongst Christians."

Once more she got the Red Cross First Aid Course under way with 27 students and a good lesson.

She includes a couple more verses of scripture: "Delight yourself also in the LORD, And He shall give you the desires of your heart."

And again: "Fear not, stand still and see the salvation of the Lord, which He will show you today."

November 23: "At 1 p.m. we had the Thanksgiving luncheon of the YWCA at the Flagler Inn. It was a real success with 165 people present, the most we have ever had."

Now at last it was time to finish with Oliver's affairs.

"On December 6 I was invited to a meeting with Mr. Johnstone of Johnstone-Higgs re my claim against Oliver Hunter's estate. For a while I thought I was going to get nothing but, in the end, he said that the Trust Company had agreed to give me $2,000.00. I had hoped for a lot more but $2,000 is better than no dollars.

"On December 11, I received my cheque for $2,000 so that is done. In the afternoon I went to the Ladies' Class, followed by a tea at the parsonage. A very pleasant day indeed."

December 18: "A friend and I had dinner and went to the Christmas concert of the Renaissance Singers held in the Ballroom of Government House. It was a delightful concert - so well done."

Over the holidays she reports a very quiet Christmas Day followed by a day of sailing with the Rushmers. "An excellent day sailing and a very good party. In the evening, a friend took me to the Buena Vista, a very swank place. I enjoyed the evening very much.

Reba - enjoying a friend's boat

December 30: Did Reba yet know that 1974 would at last open the door for her exit from the Government High School that she had been longing for? I think that she had been preparing for the move and was watching eagerly as the months from January to June passed by.

Chapter Seventeen

1974 – A Surprising End and a New Beginning

"A bend in the road is not the *end of the road*...Unless *you* fail to make the turn."

— Helen Keller

January 1974

After 16 years of challenges in her adopted land, Reba was drawing near to another new chapter in her life.

Her final year in Nassau began with more parties, church, and golf. Such was the social life of my 65-year-old cousin. These were also days of saying goodbye as more people were leaving the Island. Friends stopped by to see her before leaving for their new home in Wellington, New Zealand.

In addition to her teaching and the other activities in which she was engaged, she continued to enjoy her opportunities for teaching the Word of God to her Ladies' Class.

"On Wednesday after school I spoke to the Ladies' Class at Trinity. I spoke on the parable of the Leaven. My talk was very well received. It is truly a great pleasure to speak to these ladies. I seem to be having more inspiration for my talks in this last while."

On the other hand, while she had enjoyed the meetings of the Religious Knowledge Committee, she now found that her submission to the Religious Knowledge Committee was rejected while Sister Rita's was accepted. She decided to no longer attend.

"It is interesting how that religious experience of mine is often just turned down cold. There are certainly few people in the Christian Church today who want to have anything to do with a religion that speaks of a personal relationship with Christ. I saw so clearly in this last rejection why I could never have fitted in into the Roman Catholic Church. They have no understanding and have no desire for this religion of personal faith in Jesus. The church steps in. To me what they exalted while they rejected my efforts, was sentimental trash."

Again, we are confronted with the spiritual conflict between the evangelical faith of her youth and early ministry, the liberalism and Catholicism of the in-between years, her discomfort with the gospel preaching of Philip Norbo, and yet her ongoing commitment to a "personal relationship with Christ" which others did not understand.

But wait! In spite of her claim that she could not have fitted into the Catholic Church because of their lack of understanding of personal faith, in her retirement years she began attending mass on a weekly basis until she was shattered by the Mount Cashel scandal, but that was still in the future.

One would expect that her 65th birthday would be celebrated quite enjoyably, but her journal hardly acknowledges it.

But never fear, Muriel was here! I say that quite tongue-in-cheek for Muriel McPhee was a little red-haired bombshell, with a captivating, incessant laugh, who came from Thessalon, my hometown. She was a friend of my mother and of Reba but she landed unexpectedly, without notice.

Reba describes Muriel, "She looks funny with her cropped red hair, and her little beige cluster of curls on top of her head. The red is a very poor tint." Of course, the red came out of a bottle as it had for many a year.

To keep her entertained, she took Muriel to the racetrack, where they bet on horses named The Stranger, Wall Eye, China Doll, and Avenger. Muriel won $7.00. They went to Paradise Island looking at expensive town homes. She took Muriel to a cocktail party for the Red Cross Fair. She took her another night to a grand meal at a lady doctor's home. "The best Yorkshire pudding I have ever had."

She says, "I enjoyed having her but I wasn't too sad to see her go. She is one of those managing people who comes into one's house and takes over. She does it all in the name of being helpful, but actually, she is not considerate at all."

On March 16, school broke up for Easter holidays. She and the Rushmers sailed to Sandy Point on Abaco Island to visit her friend Max who is an unhappy headmaster there. They went in Max's boat for six hours. She caught fish, saw a shark, and a few flying fish. What a great way to spend a holiday!

The months crept by.

We've all had the kind of days or even weeks where we should have stayed in bed! On a Sunday in May 1974, so did Reba. On her way to church she was almost run over by a motor scooter. She missed part of the service because of daylight saving time. She couldn't golf because of a tournament.

On Tuesday, she got Cec Bethel to sign her application for Canadian Old Age Pension. Then on Thursday, she got one of those smug, superior letters from Geoff. She replied that she would not be coming to Ottawa this summer. An altogether forgettable week!

It was time for some fun so on Friday, she and her friend Eva went to *The Last of the Red-Hot Lovers*, a Nassau Players production, a very entertaining light comedy.

On Saturday she went to the Red Cross First Aid competition, which was to become a very good annual event.

On the next Friday she went to the Nassau Operatic Society's production, *Viva, Mexico*. "It was very amateur and not up to the productions of the past. The really good players have all left."

June 1: "It was Speech Day at the school and not only the Prime Minister, but the Minister of Education, and the secretary to the Minister of Education were present, which had not often been the case. I do feel the Holy Spirit has been with me in these instances and has really helped me."

On Thursday, she spoke to the Ladies' Class on the Prologue (Introduction) to St. John's Gospel. "The Holy Spirit was wonderfully with me and I again had a very receptive audience."

As she drew closer to her long-awaited departure from Nassau, one would expect her to be exultant but such was not the case.

June 22: "To church, then to an Anatol-sponsored staff luncheon at the Gleneagles Hotel. There was a very good lunch with all of staff present. We had a very jolly time. There were close to 70 there.

"On Tuesday, we had the end of term assembly. Very brief. Oddly enough, Anatol was very upset by my leaving. The staff meeting was brief and disjointed. In the end, Anatol couldn't speak and Keva Bethel had to finish. I came home feeling odd and disturbed."

As the writer of her story, I am thankful for this entry. Although Reba and Anatol had something of a strained relationship during Anatol's headship, I think that the two of them had a deeper friendship than perhaps either of them knew. It is quite possible that my cousin could be awkward, and sometimes show by facial expression and body language, if not in actual words, her dissatisfaction with GHS. Still, when at last that relationship is to be severed, it is noteworthy that both Reba and Anatol felt the pain of loss.

In some ways, these two women were symbolic of the overall struggle within the Bahamas. Here was a black woman taking the reins of a school and trying to steer it in the direction of a new, independent country where Bahamian culture was at the forefront and celebrated rather than stifled by the oppressing viewpoints of British rule.

Here, on the other hand was Reba, not British, and often uneasy with the outlook of the "entitled" Brits who, for too long had seen themselves as the saviours of the Bahamas. For 16 years she had straddled the divide between the two, doing her best to be a good teacher despite the difficult changes taking place around her.

As part of writing this book, I have had the privilege of communicating with Dr. Patricia Rodgers, Anatol's daughter, a delightful and highly talented woman. Patricia was a former Bahamas High Commissioner to Canada, and later to London in 1988-1992. Patricia, her sister and her brother Jonathon, an Ophthalmologist and influential leader in Nassau, are a continuing tribute to their mother and dad, Anatol and Kenneth Rodgers.

As her time in Nassau nears an end, Reba writes, "In the evening there was a small Parent-Teacher Association party - at which we were each presented with a gift from the staff and one from the Students' Council."

She reports a very great heaviness of spirit. "I feel my lonely situation very keenly. After 16 years, I am leaving Nassau. I have never been deeply attached to Nassau, so why? I don't quite understand it."

As in any of our lives, her final week was spent wrapping up the remaining details.

She sold her car. She spent time at the ministry arranging for her pension.

"On Sunday, I went to church in spite of a wicked thunderstorm. On Monday I did my last entertaining here.

"Wednesday was an exciting day. The packers came to pack the china and glass. It cost me less than $400 to get my stuff to Vancouver.

"On Friday, I went to Munn's for dinner - a real Bahamian dinner - stewed conch, grouper peas, rice and guava duff.

"Saturday involved a YWCA luncheon for myself and two others. There were about 60 present. A pleasant program. I was given an inscribed letter opener in silver. A very good and well-done event. And finally, on Sunday I went to Trinity for my final Sunday. I said my goodbyes."

Tuesday, July 23: "My last day in Nassau. I enjoyed a good dinner at a restaurant with the Rodgers. I finalized my plans and was taken to the airport. Some of the ladies came to say goodbye."

It is interesting to watch Reba in this departure from her adopted country. Sometimes we don't value what we have until the opportunity to do it is removed. Our emotional reaction is not always the proper response to a situation.

I believe Reba's time in Nassau was of greater value than she thought it was, and even in reading about it, I hope we have profited.

Her years in Nassau had brought a healing from her past experience. She had grown as a person, an independent woman who would not have had the same experience in Canada. Working in Government High School had given her a profession which continued her religious life, allowing her to share her life with others. Working with children expanded on her experience at the Children's Aid, combining and making use of her religious knowledge. Working in an entirely different culture, among a different race of people had broadened her horizons dramatically, introducing her to a world she would never have known as a minister in the United Church of Canada.

Strife in the Bahamas had gained its independence, and the struggles of her life had caused her to find her element and a kind of life she could never have had back home.

Yes, it took some time to overcome her "gaucheries", transitioning from a very conservative lifestyle into a very liberated one, but she had entered into that new element with zest and enthusiasm.

On balance, Nassau had been good for her. Now it was time to move on.

There is a sad ending to this story. On Christmas Eve, 1985, Anatol was struck by a hit and run driver and died as a result. I am certain that my cousin felt that loss very deeply.

"At 1:30 p.m., July 23, 1974, my plane left Nassau. I have had deeper feelings about leaving than I thought I would."

Chapter Eighteen

In the Steps of St. Paul

**"If you reject the food, ignore the customs, fear
the religion and avoid the people, you might better
stay home."**

— James Michener

After surprising emotions, Reba was out of Nassau. On Friday, her plane
landed in Toronto and she took the plane for Sault Ste. Marie, Ontario.
On Sunday, she and my cousin Marion attended First Baptist Church in
the Sault where Reba had a good visit with Hugh Colver who had told me
that he was led to Christ by Reba, when she was a minister in Rydal Bank,
thirty-four years previously. That must have been an interesting conversation
considering all the changes that had taken place in Reba's life since they last
saw one another.

After buying a car, visiting with family and friends, which she described as
"full and happy days," she and my mother set out to drive to British Columbia.

Along Lake Superior they drove to White River, where they heard in their
motel room President Nixon's resignation speech on August 8, 1974.

On through North Western Ontario. ("How big it is!") They passed into
Manitoba and through Winnipeg and into Saskatchewan. I wonder what her
feelings were as she drove through Peebles where she had served her student
pastorate during the summer of 1937.

Through Regina to Moose Jaw to visit Mom's sister-in law, Aggie Rowan.
They visited the area where Mom had taught school just prior to the Spanish
Flu epidemic of 1918. They also visited Mom's brother Leonard in Sylvan
Lake, Alberta.

"We drove down to Calgary and into the mountains. It was glorious. We visited the Banff Springs hotel, then to Lake Louise. At Golden, we stayed in a very expensive hotel - $15.00."

Travelling on to Vancouver, Reba again began meeting her relatives and rented a house for the winter from her cousin Louise Douglas to give her time to decide on where she wanted to be. Some great family gatherings followed.

After attending the United Church on Sunday, she had a visitor. "On Saturday Rev. Kilgour came and got an outline of my activities since leaving college. I discussed frankly my experience of going into the Roman Catholic Church." Rev. Kilgour's visit must have been helpful, for she proceeded with a membership application to the Tsawwassen United Church.

Having just arrived in Canada from Nassau followed by her long trip across the country, one would expect that she might want to settle down for a while. But no!

She was off to Vancouver Island to join her cousin Louise Miller for a trip north through Vancouver Island, mainland B.C. and Alberta.

They joined cousins Herb and Louise Douglas on the ferry, enjoying the trip north.

"It was beautiful going through the Gulf Islands. We passed Alert Bay (an Indian place) and Santula – a Swedish community. Someone led a sing-song in the evening. On Monday we docked at Prince Rupert. I was up early seeing all the waterfalls and rivers flowing into the sea. Herb and Louise left us there and returned by ferry to Vancouver. Louise Miller and I stayed over in Prince Rupert.

"On Tuesday, in spite of the fog, we got views of beautiful mountains as we followed along the Skeena River to Hazleton, a beautiful place dominated by great mountains. We got a lodge at Fraser Lake and in the morning, turned north to Chetwynd.

"We left Chetwynd with its lumber mill on our way to Fort St. John. We saw the WAC Bennett Dam and the gorge of the Peace River then on to Beaverlodge where we visited Louise's friends for a few days. I have had no part whatever in planning this journey."

Reba wanted to go to church but Louise refused. "She has a real feeling against the church. I wonder why? In this she was like her brother Geoff. This spoils her for me. I don't want friends who are against the church."

Once again, we see this interesting dichotomy. She may feel that my mother and the folk at the Thessalon Bible Chapel have a narrow, restricted religion, but she lacks respect for Louise and her brother Geoff who lack faith. As a pastor, I understand this from personal experience. Leaving Beaverlodge, they drove through Grande Prairie, through the foothills. They came out at Grand Cache, on to Hinton and Jasper. The next day they drove out to the Maligne Canyon – a natural feature located in the Jasper National Park near Jasper, Alberta.

"It was very cold on Tuesday. We had a glorious view of Mount Robson, then to Prince George as Louise was determined that I would see the Cariboo."

Through the Yellowhead Pass, they went south through Quesnel to William's Lake, south to Cache Creek and Kamloops, on to Vernon and Kalamalka Lake. She describes Kalamalka as "beautiful with its azure waters."

"From Woods Lake, we followed the lovely Lake Okanagan to Penticton where we had our final motel. On Thursday, we drove from Penticton to Vancouver. My, my house in Boundary Bay looked good to me."

In October, she began a new round of activities.

"Herb and Louise and I went to the Christian Women's Club dinner at the Hyatt Regency Hotel – a huge affair in the ballroom – over 700 in attendance. I met a couple of school principals.

"On Sunday, I was received into the membership of Tsawwassen United Church by letter of transfer. I met some new people. Then to Herb and Louise's in Richmond for a barbeque – the usual crowd. A full and very pleasant day."

She had come full circle, back to the United Church in which she once was a minister. In early October, several members of the family enjoyed a good weekend at Harrison Hot Springs. "The hotel was at the end of Harrison Lake surrounded by with great glaciers. Our unit was a bit crowded, but we enjoyed bathing in the hot pools."

On Friday, she came back to Boundary Bay. Ah, at last quiet and rest!

Nope! Just when she should be settling, the travelling bug bit her again and she was leaving on another trip, this time to Turkey and the Middle East with the Royal Athenium Cruise Line: "In the Steps of St. Paul".

In late October, 1974 she set off once again.

Is there no end to the stamina of this 65-year-old woman? We'll find out.

For those who have read the Book of Acts in the Bible and the letters of the apostle Paul in the New Testament, you will recognize that many of Paul's journeys were in Asia Minor, which we now know as the country of Turkey. His journeys took him through the Mediterranean including the Aegean Sea, Greece and Rome. This is the area to be followed on this tour - exactly what she wanted.

What a great time for us to open our Bible to the Bible maps in the back, to trace her journey. Perhaps it's even a good time to read for the first time or to read again the Book of Acts.

October 22, 1974: She arrived in Seattle to begin her flight, but there was one problem after another.

"I have never had a trip with so much to upset me."

There were problems with her passport. Her plane couldn't land so she had to stay over in Seattle for another night. She missed her connecting flight in New York but at last she got on her way.

Once more she was in a large plane on an intercontinental flight. What a contrast this plane was with its multitudes of passengers to the small Air Canada aircraft (57 passengers) in which she had flown to Nassau 17 years earlier.

"On Friday I got to Rome but did not meet my tour group who has already left so I must go on to Istanbul on my own.

"For all that, I was very thrilled getting off the plane in daylight in Asia Minor. The airport at Istanbul was very poor, like a country place. But I did meet my tour group and flew south with them to Izmir (Smyrna) where we all met our guide. We stayed in a very beautiful and very posh hotel."

Izmir is a city on Turkey's Aegean coast. Known as Smyrna in antiquity, it was founded by the Greeks, taken over by the Romans and rebuilt by Alexander the Great before becoming part of the Ottoman Empire in the 15th century.

October 26: "By 8 a.m. thirteen of us were ready with our guide Sun Kayacan for our first day of touring in Turkey. As we left Izmir on the shores of the Aegean Sea, we had a beautiful view of the Bay with the city all around and the slopes of the mountain. We passed horse-drawn wagonettes, all painted up fancy. We drove through many cotton fields. There were also olive and fig trees, empty now with the season of reaping past. The towns all had mosques with their minarets. But Sun told us that the young people have lost interest in religion."

From the 26th to the 31st they experienced a whirlwind tour of Turkey. In one day, they visited four of the cities listed in Revelation chapters 2 and 3: Pergamum, Thyatira, Philadelphia and Sardis.

"Our first ancient city was to be Pergamum. The modern town is called Pergamos and goes back as far as 3,000 B.C. In the 6th century B.C., it had connections with Alexander the Great. Then it became a Roman city. 326 A.D was the most glorious day of Pergamum. It had three theatres, one of which is excavated. The one which we visited was the steepest theatre in Asia Minor and maybe in all of the world.

"Pergamum was a great medical centre of the ancient world. In the midst of the city is an interesting block with entwined snakes on it. The physicians got poison from the snakes that they used successfully as medicine for the cure of disease. We came to a temple to the worship of Asclepios, the god of the physicians. We were shown a round dream chamber. They used definite psychological methods in those days. In fact, they had their own shock treatment. The patient would go and sit in the waterless pool. If the god favoured him and was going to cure him, he would send water to the pool. Day after day the poor man sat there, getting more and more desperate that he was not accepted by the god. Then there would be a sound of water coming. He would be so excited that he would run down the corridor, where he would hear from the ceiling a voice, 'You are healed. You are healed!' The voice would be reverberating and he would believe in the treatment with great joy.

"Pergamum was also well known for a magnificent library. They made papyrus here and later used skins for writing material. Unfortunately, at some point, the books were all taken to Egypt and burned.

"I didn't enjoy lunch, because there was a peculiar odor in the place."

She also notes that, "At Pergamum, we saw the remains of a Christian church, now used as a mosque."

I am sure that Reba was also quite familiar with the description of Pergamos in Revelation 2: 12 – 17 as the compromising church.

The second church was Thyatira. "There was little to see: only one small site with excavations. There was an old synagogue and some broken columns. The children swarmed about us. They are not very used to tourists here. We stopped at a motel for water for the bus. People were sitting at tables under the trees, but what funny toilets they have. Everything is on the floor, no seat. You squat and there is a place to put your feet. Between the feet marks is a hole. There is water to put in after using." (In future trips she became quite used to these "squat toilets.")

Once again, she may have had her Bible open to Revelation 2: 18 – 28 and its description of the corrupt church.

"Our third church was Philadelphia. Again, there is really no excavation, just two great pillars of a Byzantine church. There was a nice little Turkish garden with pomegranate trees."

She must have remembered that this church was called the faithful church in Revelation 3: 7 – 13 and given a great promise. "I know your works. See, I have set before you an open door, and no one can shut it; for you have a little strength, have kept My word, and have not denied My name…. Because you have kept My command to persevere, I also will keep you from the hour of trial which shall come upon the whole world, to test those who dwell on the earth."

"Our fourth church was Sardis. We saw first the great façade of a gymnasium, and the Sardis synagogue. We went on to see the temple of Artemis. This is the centre of the great Lydian civilization. It was getting dark, so we had to leave."

No doubt as they returned to their hotel, she had opportunity to look up the Bible's description of 'the dead church' in Revelation 3: 1 – 6.

"We returned to our hotel about 8 p.m. very tired after having had a very full day – 12 hours. We had dinner in the lovely dining room very late."

The next day, October 27, they visited Smyrna, the persecuted church. "We drove along the shore and up into the mountain on the other side. There are few ruins of the city. Alexander the Great moved the city to the top of Mount Tagus. Here we climbed onto the top of an old fortification and had a glorious view of the city of Izmir and of the location of the old city of Smyrna. On this hill the great Polycarp was burned because he refused Emperor worship. He was the bishop of Smyrna."

Refresh again your memory of the Bible's outlook on this city as recorded in Revelation 2: 8 - 11.

"From Smyrna, we drove through the countryside to Ephesus. This city was built five times on different locations. Most of the ruins are from the Roman period."

She describes Ephesus as a wonderful place with three streets all excavated. "We walked along the Arcadian Way paved with great blocks of marble. You can see where the chariot wheels made grooves in them. Each street had its separate sewage system with underground drainage. The streets were lined with statues and pillars and shops. The longest street is the Harbour Street which ran down to the sea. Today the sea is not there. It has receded 2½ miles. The silting up of the river caused commerce to fail. Earthquakes also affected the situation.

"Along one street was the fountain of Trajan How lovely it must have been. A huge great statue of Trajan

"Then up on top of the hill is the house where Paul is supposed to have lived for 2½ years. Our guide spent a lot of time showing us the baths, with hot, hotter, and hottest places – in four separate sections, also the toilets which had running water and good sewage.

"We saw the Agora paved with black and white marble. We also saw the theatre where Paul was preaching and where the uproar took place – 'Great is Diana of the Ephesians.'(Acts 19: 17 – 41.)

"We went for lunch to a native restaurant. We had chopped lamb in little rolls, vegetables as a special course and fruit.

"After lunch we went to see the Basilica of St. John. It is a very likely place for the burial of the apostle.

"Our hotel was right on the Mediterranean. We had very pleasant rooms, and the usual Turkish food for dinner. Always tomatoes and cucumbers for a salad and the fruit very often grapes."

It is sad that this church was said by Jesus to be the church which had lost its first love.

On October 28, they went on, again. Aphrodisias must have been an interesting place with its history as the home of the goddess of love. "We saw the vast hippodrome used for chariot races. It is 2,100 years old and the largest in the world. It seated thirty to forty thousand. We then visited a temple to Aphrodite and a small Christian church and the theater. We saw the concert hall which had all been made of marble. This city was the official residence of the governors. We also saw the theatre where the Christians and the gladiators entertained the people." This city is not one of the places mentioned in Revelation.

Laodicea and Colosse are two more cities of Revelation. "Almost none of Laodicea is excavated with just a few ruins to be seen but at one time this was a well populated place and a city with some very wealthy people. As we walked about, we came to a place where we could look across to a small hill, and that was Colosse, so famous in connection with Paul."

The church at Laodicea is probably one of the best-known ones because Jesus described it as the lukewarm church in Revelation 3:14 – 22.

Before we leave these seven churches, I would encourage my readers to reread these two chapters and think of the composite picture of Jesus Christ which they reveal. As I mentioned in Chapter Seven Reba had preached about these churches in Revelation. What a thrill it must have been to visit them.

I am sure that as my cousin walked the streets of these ancient churches, she was thinking of the new life awaiting her back in Tsawwassen. Having rejoined a United Church, will she now receive acceptance which had eluded her before?

On to Hierapolis, where they saw the gymnasium and a big cemetery. "We saw a fantastic white rock formation and stayed in a motel and had a swim in a pool fed by hot springs." As in other trips, they met a camel caravan, and flocks of sheep and goats on their way to the slaughterhouse. The shepherds wore sheepskins.

"We visited a cave and drove into the Taurus mountains. We saw faraway villages and a very primitive way of life."

In Perga, the theatre offered a magnificent view out to the Mediterranean Sea. They drove along the coast known as the Turkish Riviera.

As they came to Tarsus,[79] she was disappointed. The birthplace and home of the apostle Paul proved to be "a squalid city which can't be much like the home of St. Paul."

---

79 Tarsus, city, south-central Turkey. It is located on the Tarsus River, about 12 miles (20 km) from the Mediterranean Sea coast. Tarsus is an ancient city on the alluvial plain of ancient Cilicia, the birthplace of St. Paul (Acts of the Apostles 22:3). Encyclopedia Britannica

Their last day in Turkey showed them the town of Adana, before going on to Antioch where they visited a museum with lovely mosaics.

"We went up a hill to a church in a cave. It was in use in St. Paul's day, and he no doubt worshipped here."

Crossing the border to Syria, they were met by a Lebanese guide while going into Lebanon before staying at the Bristol Hotel in Beirut.

Now, here is a detour I don't understand.

Arising very early, they went to the airport and flew on Middle East Airways to Cairo. Confusion reigned. After lunch, they had a tour of Cairo. First a museum, where they saw many exhibits of King Tutankhamen, then to the pyramids, which are near to Cairo.

Reba Hern and friend - World Traveler - Egypt

A humorous incident took place. "I got on a camel and the driver wouldn't let me off until I gave him more money." I don't suppose it was so funny for her while she was on that huge animal.

"We went to one of the pyramids but it was rush, rush, down into the chamber where the mummy had been, then up through a narrow passage. I was very tired. We were driven to the Alabaster Mosque. It was beautiful with its lovely alabaster pillars. Then a visit to the bazaar. "After dinner at the hotel, we went to a Sound and Light display – a grand display of the pyramids, then a long dark trip across the desert to Alexandria, arriving at our bed on the ship at 1:30 a.m. after a long, long day."

On Saturday they left Alexandria in the dark, aboard a small, very ordinary ship, the Neptune, with one hundred fifty-three people on the cruise, mostly old folk.

"We spent most of the day at sea. We passed the Island of Crete enroute to Beirut."

Again, I ask, as I write about this, why this exhausting trip to Cairo for such little value, apart from a cruise across the Mediterranean? Her journal does not comment on that question.

November 3: "From Beirut, I opted for the tour to Damascus. We drove up into the mountains through the summer resorts on the outskirts of Beirut. Drove through a lovely well-cultivated valley to Baalbek where we saw the temple of Venus. The lowest ruins are Phoenecian, but the well-preserved ones are Roman.

"We crossed the border into Syria. Finally arrived at Damascus. We visited the beautiful Umayyad Mosque in the old city of Damascus. It is one of the largest and oldest mosques in the world. It is considered by some Muslims to be the fourth-holiest place in Islam.

"We all put on black robes and took off our shoes. We saw the supposed resting place of the head of John the Baptist.

"We drove along the street called Straight and to the place where Paul was supposed to have been let down over the wall in in a basket. Our tour ended in a lovely palace, a lovely courtyard with rooms all around it, two or three stories high. Then a long drive back through the dark to Beirut."

November 4: "Today I elected to take the trip to the Cedars of Lebanon. We drove along the shore away from Beirut where we saw some old rock carvings left by the conquerors of Lebanon. Our next stop was Byblos. Byblos was the holy place of the Phoenicians and dates back to 3,000 B.C. It was the birthplace of the alphabet. Its very name means 'the Book'. We continued along the coast, then turned inward to see the cedars. We had a glorious drive up into the mountains. We would pass a town and later look down and see it in the valley below. The road was narrow, with no guardrails.

The people living in these towns are Christians of the Maronite religion – part of Nestorianism. They are white, with fair complexions and yet there is something oriental about their villages. They have many churches and no Minarets. We drove past the town where Danny Thomas grew up. We got up to 8,000 feet and stopped at the Hotel Bernard. Above us were the highest mountains of Lebanon, some with snow on their tops. It was a beautiful place. We walked down to see at close range the Cedars of Lebanon. There are very few left. One is said to be 6,000 years old. The government has planted many of these trees but they are still not large, and they take a long time to grow."

As we read this, our minds go back three thousand years to 1 Kings 5 when King Solomon sent to Hiram about his plan to build the temple in Jerusalem. 1 Kings 5:6: "Now therefore, command that they cut down cedars for me from Lebanon; and my servants will be with your servants, and I will pay you wages for your servants according to whatever you say. For you know [there is] none among us who has skill to cut timber like the Sidonians."

Here in Lebanon, she saw evidence of the ongoing political tensions within that area: "We saw a number of tanks in these remote villages with soldiers in them."

Back on the ship travelling south: "I went out on deck at 6 a.m. and saw the coastline of Israel. I saw a gunboat rushing to meet us, but once it recognized who we were it turned back. Israel is a country at war or nearly so. How the Arabs hate Israel! We now approached Haifa as it spreads up the sides of Mount Carmel. Mount Carmel is a ridge, several miles long.

"We disembarked, got into large buses and set off for Jerusalem. Our guide was an American Israeli who now lives in Israel, so we could follow him quite well. We drove into the Valley of Jezreel, passed the city of Samaria, between Mt. Ebal and Mt. Gerazim, where Jacob's well is. We saw Mt. Gilboa in the distance, came through Ramallah, and thence to Jerusalem. Our group was placed in the National Palace Hotel, an Arab hotel – really a poor hotel."

This, of course, is the second time that she has been in Jerusalem. The first visit I recorded in Chapter Fourteen: Death – and Life.

"The next day, our buses took us on tour to the Mount of Olives and the formal Gethsemane and the church that is there. We crossed the Kidron Valley and were shown a much larger place of the Last Supper."

November 6: "We set off in the morning to tour Jerusalem. Went into the old city via the Dung Gate and visited the El Aksa Mosque. This is the third mosque of Islam, the first in Mecca, the second in Medina. The Dome of the Rock, which was our second visit, is not a proper mosque but a shrine. We did have one change from 1972. This time we went down right beside the Wailing Wall. I walked up and touched it. It was interesting to see the little pieces of paper with prayer requests pushed into the cracks.

"We then drove through an area where the orthodox Jews live. Nearly all live in apartment buildings. We drove past the Hebrew University, with 18,000 students. Now we drove out of Jerusalem through a wonderful forest, one tree planted for each of the 6,000,000 Jews slain in the last war. The trees are getting to be a good size. We saw a valley, which had long ago been the Philistine city of Ashdod. Our guide reviewed the story of the capture of the Ark of the Covenant. Big smokestacks are there now."

Once again, they left Jerusalem for the journey down to the coast. "We passed through the outskirts of Tel Aviv, barely touched on Caesarea and on to an olive wood factory. Back to Haifa and our ship where a group of singers and dancers from Israel put on a program."

November 7: "Another day of touring in Israel to Megiddo where we viewed the valley (The Valley of Har Megiddo - Armageddon). Our second stop was Nazareth with many Arabs. Certainly, the dirty place of today can have little connection with the place where Jesus lived. We went to Galilee and had lunch right on the lake. The fish was overdone, but I enjoyed the fresh dates very much. Then we all crammed into a boat for the trip to Capernaum, where we disembarked and saw a lovely kibbutz, which was begun in 1907. I was thoroughly tired out and glad to get back to the ship. Really my first trip to Israel was far superior to this."

Again, as her biographer I ask, what kind of a tour is this that rushes people through so many places and countries? Who could take in all that they have seen in such a short period of time?

November 8: "We were now told that we were to visit Cyprus. I chose to go to Paphos. We passed through marvellous grape orchards, but this war-torn country was a grim place. It can't be two months since an American ambassador was murdered here in Cyprus.

"Our first historical stop was a temple of Apollo. We saw the ruins and the theater and the place where the lions were let out to fight against the Christians.

"As we stood among the ruins, we could clearly hear big guns going off.

"We saw a white Greek town on a hill, then a very picturesque place – the birthplace of Aphrodite out at sea. Later we saw the temple of Aphrodite. The priestesses were actually prostitutes and the worship consisted of an orgy. All these places were no doubt well known to the apostle Paul and there is no doubt that he visited the Coliseum. It was good to know as we looked at the surrounding hills, that the apostle had stood here and laboured. This is the harbour from which Paul embarked and sailed to Perga.

"Returning to the ship we set sail for Rhodes. Once again, I got up early and stood on deck watching the ship come in to port at Rhodes. How interesting it was with the great Crusader castle and its walls all along the dock area.

"Getting off, we walked about the narrow streets all lined with shops. After lunch, we had a tour of the town of Lindos, a lovely white village on a slope with a steep hill behind it and a ruin on the top. This was the old city, which dates back to 700 or 800 B.C. The island was lush with many orange trees full of oranges. Lindos is a most attractive town. The steep, narrow street is all made up of small, matched cobblestones in patterns of black and white. At times along the way, a door would open and you could see into lovely, little, neat courtyards. The houses are all sparkling white.

"We got into the buses and were taken back to the ship. Certainly, this would be a lovely place for a holiday."

They were now sailing into the multitudes of islands in the Aegean Sea between Turkey and Greece. I confess that I can't find some of these places on a map.

November 10: "This morning we arrived at the island of Kos with its small, round harbour. This is not as lush a place as Rhodes but it is the second largest island of the Dodecanese, - 25 miles long – 18,000 people."

I suspect that virtually all of my readers will be as uninformed about these islands as I am. A search of www.greeka.com reveals that "The Dodecanese, in the southeastern Aegean Sea, is a group of Greek islands known for their medieval castles, Byzantine churches, beaches and ancient archaeological sites. On the largest island, Rhodes, the medieval Street of the Knights and Palace of the Grand Masters show Byzantine and Ottoman influences. Kallithéa and Ialissós are popular beach resorts, and Lindos' acropolis has panoramic coastal views."

Back to her journal: "There is a 14th century castle of the Knights of St. John here. This island is famous for early medicine: Asclepius and Hippocrates who was his son. They believed in healing by natural means. We went to the temple of Asclepius. It is believed by some that St. Luke had his training here."

Their second stop was at the Island of Patmos. As her biographer, I am very interested in her visit to this place. This, of course, was the island on which the apostle John was exiled and on which he wrote the book of Revelation. I love John's final vision, Revelation 21:1: "Now I saw a new heaven and a new earth, for the first heaven and the first earth had passed away. Also, there was no more sea."

Reba continues, "We saw the monastery on the top of a high hill, and the white town around it. We docked and all got into buses and drove part way up to the monastery, but we still had a long climb to get to the top. We went to the church where there were a number of orthodox priests. A glorious view. Patmos was larger than I thought. One island seemed to join another and it was very beautiful. When the bus was nearly down, we stopped at the cave where St. John is said to have written the Book of Revelation."

November 11: "Early we came to the island of Santrini. A great steep cliff several miles in length with white towns all along the top. There is much evidence of volcanic action here. I chose to ride to the top on a mule, a rather placid beast. (Thankfully!) How lovely these islands are with their attractive towns."

November 12: "We sailed past a number of islands, coming at last to the Island of Delos, said to be the birthplace of the Greek gods Apollo and Artemis. Delos was declared sacred to the gods.

"This tour is really superficial. Everything is rush, rush and skim over the surface. The American does not want to study things and really get to understand. He wants to pack a whole lot into as short a time as possible.

"Mykonos is a very popular tourist island. I walked the narrow streets, just room for people on foot and donkeys, but all so white and clean. It is a very attractive place."

They were now coming into Macedonia at the top end of Greece.

November 13: "From Mykonos to Thessaloniki. (1 and 2 Thessalonians) This was a city of five or six story apartment buildings all along the water. We saw a statue of Alexander the Great and drove along a street by that name. We passed the Macedonia Palace Hotel, which has 1,000 beds. 98% of the people are Greek Orthodox with no acceptance of any other church. There is a university in the city with 33,000 students. There are three different walls in the city.

"We went up to the Acropolis. We stopped at the monastery of Vlatador, but there is little or nothing left of St. Paul's time. For 400 years, the Turks were the rulers of Greece and they destroyed all the churches. We visited the Basilica of Domitian. Mostly women were at a service. We are told that few young people take an interest in the church. All the minarets have been destroyed now. We have seen plenty of Orthodox churches with their ikons and elaborate chandeliers.

"In the afternoon we all piled into the buses and set off for Pella, the birthplace of Alexander. First, we visited a museum where we saw some lovely mosaics of the ancient times. Then we were taken to see the ruins.

"From Pella, we went on to Berea. (Acts 17: 10 – 15) We saw a large stone lion near the town but there was not much excavated. There were steps Paul was said to have walked on. There was also a Byzantine church there. We returned to the ship for dinner and in the evening, a quartet came from the one evangelical church in Thessalonica. A doctor runs this church along with medical work, the only way he can work, as all evangelical Christian work is underground."

November 14: "This morning we came to Kavalla, the old Neapolis of the Bible. We set off on our trip to Philippi. (Acts 16:11 – 40) We stopped at an outlook and saw the Ignatian Way, a road well known to the apostle. One catches just glimpses of life as he might have known it. We passed through more mountainous roads and valleys and the river, which forms the border between Greece and Bulgaria. Finally, we arrived in Philippi. We walked to the swift flowing river where Paul met Lydia and the ladies at the place of prayer. It was a lovely place.

"We saw some of the ruins of Philippi, and then went to the theater and saw the place of the prison where Paul and Silas met the Philippian jailer. It was good to be in the place and to know how the apostle had laboured and suffered."

November 15: "Today our tour comes to an end, but I have elected to stay for six more days in Athens. Those of us staying were taken to our hotel while the rest were taken to the airport.

"I picked up another tour. We took a rushed trip to the Parthenon and Mars Hill. After lunch we went to the museum where we had a very poor guide. But now the fourteen or fifteen of us could go at our own pace. We drove along the shore past the summer resort places. At Cape Sunion, we went to the Temple of Poseidon. We walked about the great pillars of this storied place of Greek history. There was a great crowd on the streets since Sunday is their election and many people are having a pre-election rally."

November 16: "We again went to the Museum. This time we had an excellent guide and got so much out of the tour that it was worth repeating. We saw the modern stadium which seated 70,000 people. We drove along the Bay of Corinth. Ships were loading at a bauxite mine.

"From the Museum we walked down to the stadium where the Olympic Games had been held. No seats, just grass slopes.

"Tomorrow we return to Athens and our tour will end."

And so, she prepared to fly home. Her flight to Rome was delayed by a storm. She did get her plane and after another dismal 12 hour flight got to New York. They had to circle and circle before they could land.

On November 22, she arrived home in Vancouver.

November 26: "All Tuesday night and Wednesday morning, I was sick with a real bilious attack. I slept off and on but each time the sickness would wake me up."

After the events of 1974, it is little wonder that she was ill for a short time. What a year it had been!

One positive thing: her first pension cheque arrived from Nassau. It had been delayed three months, and she wondered if she would ever see that money but there it was.

Now she began attending the United Church in Tsawwassen regularly and reports that "I enjoy the church very much. I go to the coffee hour and always meet new people."

Chapter Nineteen

Looking Back Over a Challenging Life

"Faith is the strength by which a shattered world shall emerge into the light."

— Helen Keller

As my family experienced, Reba had a 'presence.' She was not a storyteller, as such except in writing, but what a story she had to tell! Her extensive travels had given her a breadth of knowledge of the world which is well worth sharing. As a man called Ibn Battuta has said, **"Traveling—it leaves you speechless, then turns you into a storyteller."**

But first she had to find a permanent dwelling instead of the rentals of 1975.

"It is an unpleasant experience and also a worry knowing that I must soon seek another place. As I studied for my Bible Class at the United Church, I read these good words, John 14:27, 'Peace I leave with you. My peace I give to you; not as the world gives, do I give to you. Let not your heart be troubled, neither let it be afraid.'"

Those words must have had an effect for on January 21, 1976, she wrote: "Today I had a wonderful blessing from God. A friend called to tell me of an apartment coming available on Kelly Court. No children, no pets. As I rushed to see it, I could see the wonderful hand of God in all of this, so I signed up at once."

At 67 years of age, she moved into the apartment which would be her home for the next 24 years.

When my wife and I moved from Ontario to Kamloops in 1977 to give leadership to a new church in that city, it was to this unit that we came to visit Reba from time to time. These were enjoyable visits with a woman whom we had admired but did not know very well. On some of those occasions, we stayed overnight with her, sleeping on her hide-a-bed and enjoying her company. Looking around her apartment and sharing in conversation, we gained a better knowledge of my cousin.

Noticeable were the books she was reading. I have said that she was a thinker, and the books she read demonstrated that very clearly. Books about religion. Books about politics. Books about world conditions. No doubt there were times when she knew that our ideas differed from hers but she hid her feelings well, because not until reading her journals, were we aware of what she was really thinking, even about ourselves.

Sheila and I do not remember that she said a lot about her past life. How we wish that she had shared about her childhood in Sault Ste. Marie, Ontario.

We would have been entranced to hear about her decision to go the Emmanuel College in preparation for her ground-breaking ordination as the second woman to be ordained by the United Church in Canada.

It would have been eye-opening to hear about her decision to leave 13 years of ministry and enter a convent.

How enlightening it would have been to learn about her 16 years in Nassau as the Bahamas transitioned from a British Colony to an independent member of the British Commonwealth. She could have told us so much about the escalating racial tensions that were part of a natural movement by Bahamians to throw off colonial control.

Why did we not ask her about teaching experience at the Government High School, and what it was like to teach Religious Knowledge and English to those black high school students?

There was so much more that we could have discussed. It was a failure on our part which we cannot even explain.

She had, for instance, in 1976, returned from a 60-day, seven country excursion to lands down under: Tahiti, Samoa, New Zealand, Tasmania, Australia, Singapore and Malaysia. What a trip! How I would love to explore with you her journal entries from that extensive journey.

In May and June, 1977, she toured Egypt, followed by visits to Algeria and Morocco in North Africa. In order to return home, she flew into and out of Paris, seeing in the distance Notre Dame, Sacre Coeur and the Eifel Tower.

She then flew to New York which she described as "awful" with its big lineup for immigration and thence home to B.C. by way of Montreal and Ottawa.

Those trips would have been still very fresh in her memory when we arrived in the fall of 1977. Why did we not ask about them with enthusiasm and even awe on our part? Oh, to turn back the clock!

In spite of what I said above about having a story to tell, we learned most of what I have shared with you from reading about it in her full journals rather than from any conversations with her.

From the time she arrived in the Lower Mainland, she began to get involved in a variety of groups. Having joined the United Church after coming to Tsawwassen in 1974, she was involved in the UCW - the United Church Women. She joined the University Women's Club, the Canadian Women's Club, the Christian Women's Club, the Opera Club and the Hospital Auxiliary.

She was on the executives of some of these organizations. She went to meetings of the Full Gospel Business Men's Fellowship. She went to the Opera, and special theatre productions. She attended a variety of churches: St David's Anglican Church, the Presbyterian Church and the 10th Avenue Alliance, and even the Baptist Church. And of course, there was a steady round of activities with her relatives. Her weeks were full!

One night, my wife received a phone call from Reba to tell her that through the University Women's Club, she had won a three day stay at the Hotel Vancouver. She thought that we could use that mini-holiday more than she could. What a surprise!

When we arrived at the hotel, we found that we were put in an amazing suite of rooms, and with dinner in the Timber Room. My, three nights in luxury. That was more than this pastor and his wife were used to.

Yes, she was a generous woman and a busy one.

There creeps in, though, a different note. In a letter, she speaks of her rejection at the Tsawwassen United Church.

"Everyone said that I would be the first woman elder but I was not selected. Instead, two other women were put in as elders. I was completely ignored. The same thing happened in the Sunday School. Again, I agreed to teach a course for their teachers. Once again, I was ignored. After I left their church, not a single person called or expressed the fact that I was missed. They were quite happy to let me go for I was a threat to them.

"So, I have cut my ties with the United Church. The teaching of the United Church has undermined the authority of the scriptures. It has sapped the faith right out of that church. It is a hopeless situation."

She no longer attended the UCW.

She became increasingly disenchanted with other things in coming years. She found the Christian Women's Club catered mostly to younger women. "I am now finishing my term of office. I don't enjoy this organization at all. They are all so self-centred and so very introspective. Their witness for Christ is 'See what a happy bunch we are. Don't you long to join us?' It is not Christ at all, but what God has done for us! I am so tired of this self-centred Christianity, but I have learned to shut up and they have no idea of my feelings."

Having left the United Church, Reba turned to St. David's Anglican Church. Writing several years later she says, "My final attempt at getting into a church here in Tsawwassen was St. David's Anglican. At first there seemed to be a very great spiritual power at work in this church. The rector held Bible studies each Thursday a.m. I attended because it was considered that a real renewal of the Holy Spirit was taking place. I had no idea of being a leader.

"In this group was a woman who assisted the rector in serving communion who also laid hands on people who came for prayer. I sensed hostility to me at once. I was a threat to her. Her Christianity was based on personal experience with minimal knowledge of scripture. She didn't believe there was a personal devil. This spiritual movement was on shaky ground - based on personal experience, not devotion to our Lord."

A change of rectors didn't help. The new man was of a Pentecostal background and wanted to turn the church into a more Pentecostal style. The old time Anglicans left. "Another woman pushed herself into leadership until she left her husband and took up with another man."

She left that church too.

In the years that followed she continued to travel extensively which is the subject for another book.

She also experienced a great deal of frustration and even disillusionment with various churches and the Christian religion during a time of great upheaval (the United Church's response to questions of divorce, moral issues and inclusion, while the Roman Catholic Church tried to deal with the Mount Cashel scandals). These are also a separate story.

In August of 1988, she wrote, "As the fall comes on, I have decided to drop three groups. I will drop completely the Christian Women's Club. I will drop being a volunteer with the Hospital Association. I will drop the United Church Women."

None of this took place without a certain regret. "In a way, I felt sad for I like being on executives and being president, but under the circumstances there was no choice."

Reba Hern in Retirement - 1974 - 2000

Having never married, she had time to ponder life to a degree which most people don't have time for, as we wrestle with home life, raising families, maintaining employment and other normal life demands. Being so often on the cusp of change. she was able to observe changes first hand more than most of her contemporaries.

In addition to books, she read the newspaper - the Vancouver Sun and political columns.

Her journals became full of commentary about Canadian and U. S. politics, especially her dislike of Ronald Reagan of the U.S. and Brian Mulroney of Canada.

I don't want to leave the impression that she only read and thought about politics. There is evidence that she was reading her Bible, writing notes and Bible studies on numerous passages. She struggled with her understanding of many things. She wrote out many passages of scripture from both Old and New Testaments to answer the question: "Who was Jesus of Nazareth?" She seemed to prefer this designation to other titles.

Her journals reflect a great deal of concern over the Protestant faith in general and Evangelical Christianity in particular.

She feels that those of us who claim to be evangelicals are all setting ourselves up as superior beings. 'You have to become like me!' She uses this as an illustration of what she claims to be the great weakness of Protestantism. "These folks want to be people of importance. They set themselves up as guides to other people."

"Indeed," she says, "I have that problem in my own life but it doesn't work. It turns far more people away from Christ than it draws to Him."

Reba is not the only person with this view of evangelicals, especially of Baptists. There is a very strong feeling that the claim to 'being saved', being forgiven of all our sin because Jesus took our sin upon Himself on the cross, makes us self-righteous, feeling that we are better than others. In fact, the opposite is true. Christianity has made us aware of how far short of the mark we fall, with no hope at all apart from Christ's mercy and grace. If He does not forgive us, we have no hope whatever. In reality, this is the very message that Reba herself once preached.

Nevertheless I, myself, her cousin and the author of this biography did not escape her criticism. We have already seen in earlier chapters that she looked upon the Brethren Assembly in which my mother and I had found wonderful Christian teaching as narrow and unattractive.

Later in 1984, my brother Gordon called me to ask me to come home. My brothers felt that my 89-year-old mom should no longer live alone but move to the Algoma Manor. They felt that I, as the white-haired boy, should come and convince mom to make this move. We made the trip, and I urged mother that the time had come to enter the Care Home, in order to get more help. She did not take it well. She was very upset.

What I didn't know was how Reba perceived this till reading her journal.

"Taking his place as the leading person in the family, he went to Aunt Mabel and insisted that she sign the papers for admission which she did. Later she realized what Allen had forced her to do and felt that this was the ultimate rejection of her. I couldn't help but re-evaluate Allen as a person," says Reba. "How can he have the love of God in his heart and reject his old mother like this?" In this, my cousin was completely mistaken.

It is at this period and set against this background, that Reba was turning more and more to the Roman Catholic church. She was now attending weekly mass in Catholic churches and finding comfort in 'the Blessed Sacrament.'

"The great weakness of the Protestant Church is that it has thrown over the sacrament and put in its place the preaching of the Word which each man interprets the Bible in His own way. "Human reason is on the throne. Our Lord knew what He was doing when He laid down the Blessed Sacrament as the foundation of the church and baptism as the way in. When the Protestants revolted, they gave up too much. In their efforts to discredit the Catholics, they gave up the heart and core of Jesus' teaching - the Blessed Sacrament. Each person is a law unto himself."

As one of those Protestants whom she criticized, I disagree with this opinion and indeed, she herself later came to the point where she disagreed with it, especially when the church was caught up in the Mount Cashel scandal.

Of that, she wrote, "My faith is being very badly shaken in the Catholic church. I can't accept it. Well, I guess I will keep on going to the Catholic church because there is nothing better, but I am afraid my heart is no longer in western Christianity. I have lost a great big slice of my respect and confidence in the Catholic Church. Something has gone that will not return."

So, what do you do when your whole world, all your ideals, all your dreams and aspirations lie shattered around your feet? That was what the Mount Cashel scandal did to Reba Hern. I am sure that it also had the same effect on many others.

As we read Reba's journals, we were surprised to find that they revealed her criticisms of myself so you can understand my amazement when, in her last year, she appointed me as her executor!

You can see from this chapter that my cousin, in her retirement years was often deeply conflicted. But none of this can detract from the qualities of this unusual woman. In spite of being so often distressed by the challenge and change which she experienced, there is no doubt in my mind that she truly trusted the Lord Jesus and was a true child of God even through her most confusing times.

She was, throughout her life, a strong, independent woman, in many ways, a woman ahead of her time.

Her last journal ends with this hymn, which addresses her deepest desires.

Lead on, O King Eternal,
The day of march has come;
Henceforth in fields of conquest
Thy tents shall be our home.
Through days of preparation
Thy grace has made us strong;
And now, O King Eternal,
We lift our battle song.

Lead on, O King Eternal,
Till sin's fierce war shall cease,
And holiness shall whisper
The sweet amen of peace.
For not with swords' loud clashing,
Nor roll of stirring drums;
With deeds of love and mercy
The heav'nly kingdom comes.

Lead on, O King Eternal,
We follow, not with fears,
For gladness breaks like morning
Where'er Thy face appears.
Thy cross is lifted o'er us,
We journey in its light;
The crown awaits the conquest;
Lead on, O God of might.

CHAPTER 20

Free At Last!

**"For I consider that the sufferings of this present time
are not worthy to be compared with the glory which
shall be revealed in us."**

— The Bible: Romans 8:18

On Sunday night, November 12, 2000, my wife and I received a visit at our home in Kelowna, from an RCMP officer. He came to tell us that Reba had been found dead in her apartment. She was 91 years of age. A brain hemorrhage had taken her life. This must have caught her completely by surprise. She did not expect to pass from this life so soon.

Going into her apartment was a shock. She was not there! We went into an empty apartment, left essentially as she had been living in it on that final day.

What were we to do? Where were we to start?

Finding her will, we began the process by which we could take charge of her affairs. A visit to her Notary Public helped. A death certificate and confirmation of myself as her executor allowed us access to her bank accounts, safety deposit box and other needed information. A visit to the funeral home established a time for Reba's memorial service on November 28.

Back in Kamloops, we picked up my brother and his wife at the airport as they arrived from Ontario. I had the pleasure of having my oldest brother in our Kamloops church as I preached morning and evening on Sunday the 26th.

On Monday we drove to Tsawwassen, ready to preach Reba's service on Tuesday at the Delta Funeral Chapel.

There was not a large gathering: simply some of her relatives, my brother and sister-in-law and a few friends. My brother Norman gave his memories of Reba. He had known her thirteen years longer than I had, for he had been 11 years old when Reba began her ministry. I had not yet been born.

Now it was my time to preach her funeral service. After such a varied life, what message would summarize the challenges and the many changes of my cousin's long life? At that point I had not read her 40 journals, so I did not know of all her struggles moving from church to church, to a convent, to the Bahamas, to the world.

Let me share with you what I said that morning:

As part of my introduction I said, "One thing I am sure that we are all glad for was the clarity of mind that Reba enjoyed up to the moment of her death. Reba lived alone but she kept her mind active through constant reading and she was well informed and able to discuss almost any subject.

"Hers has been a varied life, including courage and boldness, at times conflict and confusion in which the way ahead had not always been clear.

"Thinking of that, I was led to 1 Corinthians 13:12: "For now we see in a mirror, dimly, but then, face to face. Now I know in part, but then I shall know just as I am also known."

"This passage tells us that:

1. **Life is not always easy to understand. 'Now we see in a mirror, dimly,'**

   "I am sure that many of us have found many things in life that we did not fully understand as they have happened to us. I have a feeling that such was the case for Reba Hern.

   "I have no doubt at all of her genuine faith in the Lord and of her desire to please Him. Norman has told us of listening to her preach, and of her commanding presence and strong delivery. I believe that she had a clear witness to the truth of the gospel.

   "Yet who knows what pressures she faced as a young woman minister? I am sure that much soul searching was involved in the decision to leave the ministry, enter a convent and later secure a teaching position in Nassau, the Bahamas, where she taught for years until she retired and moved to Tsawwassen where she has lived out the remainder of her life.

   "No, life is not always easy to understand but:

2. **There is a day of perfect understanding just ahead. "Now we see in a mirror, dimly, but then, face to face."**

"For the believer in Jesus Christ, death is not a threat. Paul said in another place, "For I have a desire to depart and to be with Christ which is far better." Whatever the confusions of this life they will all be swept away in glory, for at last we shall see Jesus face to face, and all will be clear. Many things we could not understand here will be seen with perfect clarity there, for then we shall see things through God's eyes. All Reba's questions about various churches and religions will now be answered.

"This is needed because:

3. **Even at its best our present knowledge is imperfect. "Now I know in part,"**

"We like to think we have a handle on life. We like to think that education and experience has given us a good knowledge of many subjects.

"Reba was a voracious reader. She did not do a lot of light reading. She loved books that challenged and enlarged her thinking. Along with that she was an ardent reader of the scriptures and books about the scriptures. She gave me a couple of her books and they had notes written all through them. Her journals are full of references to various passages from the Bible.

"One of her special joys in these retirement years has been her continuing travels to many lands. How she loved to share the sights she saw and the people she went with on those trips.

"But no matter how much we study our knowledge is "in part".

4. **There is a glorious day with perfect knowledge. "but then I shall know as I am known."**

"It has been a few years since Reba has taken one of her trips to foreign lands, but two weeks ago she took the greatest trip of all her life, for she took the trip from earth to heaven; from the world of sense to the world of Spirit, and from the limitations of the flesh to the full knowledge of the Lord. Think of the implications of that statement: "I shall know as I am known." In this life we have not had perfect knowledge of God, but God has had perfect knowledge of us. When we enter that realm of glory and see our Saviour face to face, our knowledge will be complete. Small wonder we sing, "What a day, glorious day, that will be!"

"Do you have that assurance? Are you looking forward with anticipation to that day? Not everyone will be in heaven. There is only one way to be there and that is through turning in faith to the Lord Jesus Christ. Amen." I hope that message rang true for many of the people who were at her memorial service. I hope that it rings true for my readers today.

It was Reba's will to be buried with her family in the cemetery near my home town, so Norman and Jean took the lovely urn containing her remains with them on the plane and buried them beside her parents in Thessalon, Ontario.

In her will she chose to leave her entire estate to the Canadian Blind Mission which I am sure helped them to carry on their work.

A delight was to give her excellent quality bed to a woman who badly needed it. She was thrilled to receive it.

As we were cleaning out her apartment, we found many photograph albums, her passports and her many journals from which I have quoted extensively. These covered her early life as a 16-year-old, her years in Nassau, her travels to many parts of the world, and her life after retirement. I wish very much that she had written about her years of ministry. As we glanced through those journals, the thought that came clearly to mind was "Here is a story worth telling." She was quite a woman, was my cousin Reba! As mentioned earlier, she entered each phase of her life at the very moment of major change:

- as a sixteen-year-old in 1925, at the formation of the United Church of Canada;
- as a twenty-eight-year-old at the ordination of women to United Church ministry in 1936 and 1938;
- as a forty-eight-year-old, coming to the Bahamas at the very start of the struggle for change of government from colonial to black rule and independence from British rule in 1957-1973.

Certainly, her years in retirement from 65 years to 91 years were lived in a period of major social change here in Canada and the western world.

Although, especially in later years, she might have rejected the idea, she joined Lydia Gruchy as a pioneer in the women's movement in becoming the second woman ordained into ministry. Certainly, she was a pioneer under constant scrutiny of those determined to prove that she did not belong.

Her choice to go to Nassau as an independent, single woman, making a new home in a country which was seeking its own independence was courageous. Finding an outlet for her faith as a teacher of religious knowledge was an outgrowth of that courage.

Her extensive travels to all parts of the world, without a travelling companion, or with the responsibility for an elderly companion falling upon her own shoulders, again mark her out as a brave and fearless adventurer.

Even her struggles as she evaluated and assessed the different religious currents of Canada in the seventies, eighties and nineties caused her to stand alone. Though her conclusions may have been flawed, leading to her deep disappointment and disillusionment, she was nonetheless a fascinating woman. As our nieces and nephews said, "She had a presence."

During her lifetime she often experienced a clash of different viewpoints, and although she learned to keep her views to herself, her journals clearly reveal the truth that an inscrutable exterior did not remove her strong personal opinions.

I don't know whether the story I have shared with you is what she would have wished me to say. Perhaps she would feel exposed by my bringing out things which she probably never intended for publication. After all, in spite of having far more information about her in her own words than we normally have for any person, her life contains many mysteries about which we will never know the answer. I hope that were she able to read this story as you have done, she would be pleased.

One thing is clear. She is free at last. In heaven she now lives in the presence of Jesus of Nazareth, the eternal Son of God. She now understands things which were unclear during her lifetime and one day, when Jesus steps off that eternal throne and returns for His own, (John 14:3, and 1 Thessalonians 4:13-18), bringing with Him all those who sleep in Jesus, she, along with all those who belong to Him will receive her new body, perfectly prepared for her life in the new heavens and new earth - forever!

Way to go Reba. You were not always right. You were not always understood, but the joys and travails of your life certainly did reveal to us a complex and thoroughly interesting and intriguing woman.

One final word of scripture which is fitting for her life of challenge and change:

> **"For I consider that the sufferings of this present time are not worthy to be compared with the glory which shall be revealed in us."** Romans 8:18.

Amen.

Challenge and Change - The Travails and Joys of a Complex Woman

By Allen Hern

About the Book:

Challenge and Change: The Travails and Joys of a Complex Woman is a celebration and exploration of the life of Reba Hern—the second woman in all of Canada to be ordained into the United Church ministry, a strong, independent woman who stepped outside the box, breaking ground for others through a wide variety of experiences and numerous major world events—a woman ahead of her time.

After thirteen years of ministry, Reba burned out and entered a Catholic Convent for five years, following which, this native of Sault Ste Marie, ON, travelled to Nassau, Bahamas where she spent the next sixteen years teaching Religious Knowledge and English in the Government High School.

During that time, Reba was on hand for the birth of a black government and for the Independence of the Bahamas from British Colonial rule. From this position, she began to travel the world, a recreation she continued after retiring to Tsawwassen, BC, in 1974.

Challenge and Change illustrates the degree to which opportunities for women have progressed since WW II and investigates these questions: How did women secure the right to become ministers in a profession which had traditionally been male dominated? What was it like for a white woman to live and teach black students in a predominately black culture? What was the country of the Bahamas like? How did the Bahamas achieve its independence? What is it like to travel in countries in which English is a secondary language or where bathroom facilities consist of a hole in the floor?

About the Author:

Pastor Allen Hern, Reba's cousin and the author of this book, was Reba's executor and preached her funeral sermon. At the time of her death at 91 years of age in the year 2000, Reba had filled forty journals with her cramped hand-writing. These became the basis for *Challenge and Change: The Travails and Joys of a Complex Woman*. To assist him in writing this book, Pastor Hern and his wife visited Nassau, meeting professors in the University and others who knew Reba personally or were able to help him research.

Also by Allen Hern is the biography of his parents (and himself): *A Good Heritage - the story of Lew and Mabel Hern,* published in 2020.

Pastor Hern and his wife, Sheila, live in Kamloops, BC. They have been in British Columbia for forty-four years after arriving from Ontario in 1977. Together they have had two pastorates in Ontario and five in BC.